GEORGE LANGE

Mark Epstein, M.D., is a psychiatrist in private practice in New York City who lectures frequently about the value of Buddhist meditation for psychotherapy. His previous books include *Thoughts Without a Thinker, Going to Pieces Without Falling Apart,* and *Going on Being.* He has written for *Tricycle: The Buddhist Review, Yoga Journal,* and *O: The Oprah Magazine.*

Also by Mark Epstein

GOING ON BEING

GOING TO PIECES WITHOUT FALLING APART

THOUGHTS WITHOUT A THINKER

OPEN TO DESIRE

The Truth about What the Buddha Taught

MARK EPSTEIN, M.D.

GOTHAM BOOKS

GOTHAM BOOKS
Published by Penguin Group (USA) Inc.
375 Hudson Street, New York, New York 10014, U.S.A.

Penguin Group (Canada), 90 Eglinton Avenue East, Suite 700, Toronto, Ontario,
Canada M4P 2Y3 (a division of Pearson Penguin Canada Inc.); Penguin Books Ltd, 80
Strand, London WC2R 0RL, England; Penguin Ireland, 25 St Stephen's Green, Dublin
2, Ireland (a division of Penguin Books Ltd); Penguin Group (Australia), 250
Camberwell Road, Camberwell, Victoria 3124, Australia (a division of Pearson
Australia Group Pty Ltd); Penguin Books India Pvt Ltd, 11 Community Centre,
Panchsheel Park, New Delhi - 110 017, India; Penguin Group (NZ), Cnr Airborne and
Rosedale Roads, Albany, Auckland, New Zealand (a division of Pearson New Zealand
Ltd); Penguin Books (South Africa) (Pty) Ltd, 24 Sturdee Avenue, Rosebank,
Johannesburg 2196, South Africa

Penguin Books Ltd, Registered Offices: 80 Strand, London WC2R 0RL, England

Published by Gotham Books, a division of Penguin Group (USA) Inc.
Previously published as a Gotham Books hardcover edition.

First trade paperback printing, January 2006

10 9 8 7 6 5 4 3 2 1

The Library of Congress has cataloged the hardcover edition of this title as follows:
Epstein, Mark, 1953–
      Open to desire : embracing a lust for life : insights from
   Buddhism & psychotherapy / Mark Epstein.
         p. cm.
      Includes bibliographical references.
      ISBN 1-592-40108-2 (hardcover) ISBN 1-592-40185-6 (paperback)
         1. Desire—Religious aspects—Buddhism. 2. Desire—Psychological aspects.
   3. Psychotherapy—Social aspects. 4. Buddhism—Doctrines.
   5. Reality principle (Psychology) I. Title.
   BQ4430.D47E67 2005
   294.3'44—dc22   2004053920

Printed in the United States of America
Set in Dante MT
Designed by Lynn Newmark

Earlier versions of some of the material in this book have previously appeared in *Yoga Journal* and *O: The Oprah Magazine*.

Grateful acknowledgment is made for permission to reprint the following:
An excerpt from "Craving" from *The Dhammapada*. Copyright, P. Lal, Writer's Workshop, 162/92 Lake Gardens, Calcutta, India 7004S

Selections from William Buck's *Ramayana*, copyright © 1976 by the Regents of the University of California. Reprinted by permission of University of California Press, Berkeley, California.

Selection from Miranda Shaw's *Passionate Enlightenment: Women in Tantric Buddhism*, copyright © 1994 by Princeton University Press. Reprinted by permission of Princeton University Press, Princeton, New Jersey.

Selections from *On Wings of Awe (A Machzor for Rosh Hashanah and Yom Kippur)*, edited and translated by Rabbi Richard N. Levy, copyright © 1985 B'nai B'rith Hillel Foundation. Reprinted by permission of the B'nai B'rith Hillel Foundation, Washington, D.C.

for Arlene

Contents

Acknowledgments

This book could not have been written without conversations with and support from the following people: John House, Nadine Helstroffer, George Lange, Rob Stein, Alex McNear, Michael Vincent Miller, Barbara Boris, Michael Eigen, Emmanuel Ghent, Daniel Goleman, Sharon Salzberg, Robert Thurman, Elizabeth Cuthrell, Joseph Goldstein, Jody Shields, Mickey Lemle, Cyndi Stivers, Janine Antoni, Kathleen Tolan, Ann Epstein, Bernard Edelstein, Larry Brilliant, Catherine Ingram, David Lichtenstein, Stephen Batchelor, Martine Batchelor, Kiki Smith, Carroll Dunham, Neil Gordon, Ed Rothfarb, Lisa Gornick, Ken Hollenbeck, Krishna Das, John Bush, Amy Gross, Fred Sandback, Mohani Dindial, Genine Lentine, Jeffrey Hoffeld, Carol Hoffeld, Marion Stroud, Jack Kornfield, Richard Alpert, Franklin Epstein, Sherrie Epstein, Jean Shechet, David Shechet, Marilyn Robie, Arthur Shechet, Sonia Epstein, Will Epstein, Ellie Shechet, Ben Shechet, Anne Edelstein, William Shinker, Lauren Marino, Margery Cantor, Emilie Stewart, Jeffrey Hopkins and Arlene Shechet. My patients have generously shared their inner lives with me and provided material for this book; in all cases cited herein, I have changed names as well as other identifying details, or constructed composites, in order to protect privacy.

"There's no prayer like desire."

Tom Waits

Introduction

The Baby and the Bathwater

One of my favorite stories comes from the Sufi tradition of mystical Islam. It is a tale that tells us exactly what we will have to face if we endeavor to walk the path of desire. A man sits in the center of a Middle Eastern marketplace crying his eyes out, a platter of peppers spilled out on the ground before him. Steadily and methodically, he reaches for pepper after pepper, popping them into his mouth and chewing deliberately, at the same time wailing uncontrollably.

"What's wrong, Nasruddin?" his friends wonder, gathering around the extraordinary sight. "What's the matter with you?"

Tears stream down Nasruddin's face as he sputters an answer. "I'm looking for a sweet one," he gasps.

It is one of Nasruddin's most endearing qualities that he

speaks out of both sides of his mouth. Like desire itself, teaching stories about Nasruddin always have two aspects. Nasruddin is a fool, but he is also a wise man. There is an obvious meaning to his actions, containing one kind of teaching, and a hidden meaning, containing another. The first meaning jumps out from the story right away. It is the basic message of both Buddhism and Freudian theory. Desire never learns; it never wakes up. Even when eliciting nothing but suffering, it perseveres. Our indefatigable pursuit of pleasure keeps us doing some awfully strange things.

Certainly, Nasruddin is modeling our lives for us: Struggling against the tide of disappointment, we continue to search for a sweet one. As his friends must be wondering as they gaze at him incredulously, would it not be better just to give up? In this version of the story, Nasruddin is rendering a conventional spiritual teaching. Our desires bind us to the wheel of suffering. Even though we know that they bring us pain, we cannot convince ourselves to relinquish our grip. As Freud liked to say, there is an "unbridgeable gap"[1] between desire and satisfaction, a gap that is responsible for both our civilization and our discontent.

But Nasruddin's perseverance is a clue to how impossible it is to abandon ship. He is an enlightened teacher, after all, not just a fool. Like it or not, he is saying, desire will not leave us alone. There is a hopefulness to the human spirit that will just not accept no for an answer. Desire keeps us going, even as it takes us for a ride. As Freud was also fond of saying, desire "presses ever forward unsubdued,"[2] pushing us to find and make use of our creativity, propelling us toward an elusive but nonetheless compelling goal.

Nasruddin's parable models the solution to desire's insatiability as well as the problem. His desire is undeterred, despite the anguish that it brings. In his unself-conscious weeping, in his implicit acceptance of both the perils and the promises of longing, lies a hidden wisdom in relationship to desire's relentless demands. Nasruddin makes no apologies for his desire; it persists unperturbed despite his apparent suffering. Nor does he fight with his tears in an effort to make them go away. Both sadness and longing are left undisturbed. Though cognizant of his own folly, Nasruddin does not desist. He seems to know that, despite his tears, there is pleasure that comes in the looking.

I am drawn to this story because of the way it embodies both the disturbing and the compelling nature of desire. As a psychiatrist and psychotherapist, I am confronted every day with clients whose stories resemble Nasruddin's. Over and over again, they engage in behaviors that from any rational standpoint they should abandon. Their frustrations spill out in my office like Nasruddin's tears. I am tempted, at times, to respond as Nasruddin's friends do. "Why not just stop?" I want to say to them. "Why not just throw in the towel?" As a therapist who has been influenced not just by the insights of psychodynamic theory but also by the wisdom of Buddhist psychology, it would be easy for me to take this position. One reading of Buddha's teachings certainly suggests that the only solution to neurotic misery lies in forsaking desire altogether. Much of Eastern thought is based upon the idea that renunciation is the key to spiritual and psychological growth. "Why search for pleasure if that search is the cause of suffering?" ask many teachers from the East. But over the years I have come to appreciate that, while there is a time and a place for this kind of logic, desire can be an important ally as well as a foe.

IN DEFENSE OF DESIRE

In thirty years of trying to integrate the psychological wisdom of East and West, desire has become for me the pivotal concept that links the two, the fulcrum upon which they both rest. When I first discovered Buddhism, I was taken with its no-nonsense appraisal of the human condition. "All life is suffering," the Buddha taught in the first of his Four Noble Truths. Physical illness and mental illness are suffering; not to obtain what one desires is suffering; to be united with what one dis-likes or separated from what one likes is suffering; even our own selves—never quite as substantial as we might wish them to be—are suffering. When I learned that the word that the Buddha used for suffering, *dukkha*, actually has the more subtle meaning of "pervasive unsatisfactoriness," I was even more im-pressed. "Suffering" always sounded a bit melodramatic, even if a careful reading of history seemed to support it. "Pervasive un-satisfactoriness" seemed more to the point. Even the most pleasurable experiences are tinged with this sense of discontent because of how transient and insubstantial they are. They do not offset the insecurity, instability and unrest that we feel.

The Buddha's Second Noble Truth, of the cause, or "aris-ing," of *dukkha* is traditionally translated as "The cause of suf-fering is desire." While I now appreciate that this is a mistranslation, it is still the most common understanding of the Buddha's insight. Desire, and all that it connotes, have taken on quite negative connotations for many of those who are drawn to Buddhist thought. In the first decade of my involvement with Buddhism, as I traveled to Asia, did many silent meditation retreats and immersed myself in the nascent Buddhist culture then springing up in the West, I witnessed a general valorization of the state of "having no preferences," a demonization of desire. The world is not a problem for a person with no preferences, we told each other, echoing an overlooked and then rediscovered novel by a contemporary of Freud's, Robert Musil, called *The Man Without Qualities*.

Upending the usual way of approaching desire in our culture, which is to indulge it either mindlessly or guiltily, this "counter"cultural perspective seemed, at first, fresh and inspired. Putting aside the conventional rush toward comfort and security opened up time and space for spiritual contemplation. However, in actual fact, it often degenerated into a group of people unable to decide where to go or what to do. Even going out to a restaurant posed insurmountable problems. "You decide," one person might say. "It really doesn't matter," another might reply, and a general paralysis would result with no person willing to reveal his or her true preferences. Apathy ruled. For want of desire, life's vitality began to evaporate.

The problem with denying any aspect of the self is that it persists as a shadow. Clearly, it is not possible to eliminate desire by pretending it is not there. It resurfaces, insistently, as Freud indicated in his famous phrase, "The return of the repressed." With a regularity that has been mirrored in more traditional Western religious communities, those who believed they were stronger than their desires were proven wrong. As the French say, *"Chassez le naturel, il revient au galop."* Chase away the natural, and it comes back at a gallop.

OPEN TO DESIRE

When I began to work as a psychotherapist, after completing many years of medical and psychiatric training undertaken after my introduction to Buddhism, I discovered how important it was to be able to admit to, or "own," one's desires. Freud's initial emphasis in psychoanalysis, in fact, was all about helping people plagued with forbidden desires. Psychotherapy, in the hands of Freud and his followers, became a means of allowing people to close the gap between their wishful conception of themselves and who they really were. More often than not, this meant learning to accept and tolerate wishes and urges from which a person had become estranged. As I began to treat my own patients, I was given a special window into the particular struggles of those engaged in a spiritual path. Because of my immersion in Buddhist thought, many of those who sought me out for therapy were themselves drawn to the spiritual. In fact, one of the things I was struck by was how prodigiously people had been using the Eastern spiritual traditions to try to serve a therapeutic function. With my own patients, I was privileged to see how fundamental the issues of desire remained, even after years of spiritual pursuit. What I observed has led me to write this book.

Many sincere people drawn to Eastern spirituality are in danger of throwing the baby out with the bathwater. In identifying the cause of suffering as desire, they struggle to eliminate it from their being. A number of these people have come to consult me, wondering why their spiritual pursuits have not brought them the peace of mind they were expecting. To sit with them in a room is to feel people not quite at peace with themselves. There can be a closed, anxious or fearful quality underlying the way they express themselves. When they become more honest about their desires, a different feeling emerges. They become more present, alive, open and tender. The brittleness disappears. It becomes easier to breathe. All of the feelings that I associate with meditation, that I want to make accessible to people through the medium of psychotherapy, open up when people become able to treat their desires as their own.

This is why the story of Nasruddin has such poignancy for me. As he defiantly indicates, there is more to desire than just suffering. There is a yearning that is as spiritual as it is sensual. Even when it degenerates into addiction, there is something salvageable from the original impulse that can only be described as sacred. Something in the person (dare we call it a soul?) wants to be free, and it seeks its freedom any way it can. This is one of the major insights to have precipitated out of my study of the psychologies of East and West. *There is a drive for transcendence that is implicit in even the most sensual of desires.* While there are certainly currents in both Eastern and Western spiritual traditions that dismiss or denigrate desire, encouraging us to forsake it through renunciation or sublimation, there is another, more controversial, alternative that Nasruddin points to in his story and that I have found necessary in helping my patients.

Known in the East as the *tantric*, or "left-handed" path, desire, in this view, is a vehicle for personal transformation. It is a yoga in its own right. Rather than treating it as the cause of suffering, desire is embraced as a valuable and precious resource, an emotion that, if harnessed correctly, can awaken and liberate the mind. In this way of thinking, desire is the human response to the discontent described in the Buddha's First Noble Truth. It is the energy that strives for transcendence but, if it is to truly accomplish its goals, the seeker must learn to relate to it differently. He or she must learn how to use desire instead of being used by it. In this sense, desire is the foundation for all spiritual pursuits. As a well-known contemporary Indian teacher, Sri Nisargadatta, famous for sitting on a crowded street corner selling inexpensive *bidis*, or Indian cigarettes, once commented, "The problem is not desire. It's that your desires are too small."[3] The left-handed path means opening to desire so that it becomes more than just a craving for whatever the culture has conditioned us to want. Desire is a teacher: When we immerse ourselves in it without guilt, shame or clinging, it can show us something special about our own minds that allows us to embrace life fully.

THE NATURAL

When the Buddha taught his First Noble Truth, he elaborated the gnawing sense of incompleteness that underlies much of our experience. As if he were describing the Second Law of Thermodynamics (that every isolated thing is moving toward a more disorganized state) or Freud's reality principle (that pleasure cannot be maintained indefinitely but must always give way to unpleasure), the Buddha evoked the unrest, instability and uncertainty that color our lives. In the face of these qualities, which he called the three *marks* of existence, we all feel yearning or longing. In the psychodynamic world, this yearning or longing is sometimes described, in the language of the psychoanalyst Melanie Klein, as the *depressive position*. In the curious reverse language of psychoanalysis, the depressive position is considered a developmental achievement because it acknowledges the feelings that come with an acceptance of separateness. The ability to see things the way they are, not to expect constant gratification but to understand that all things are limited, is what allows for personal growth.

Desire is a natural response to the reality of suffering. We feel incomplete and desire completeness; we feel unrest and desire ease; we feel insecurity and desire comfort; we feel alone and desire connection. Our experience of life, our very personalities, are shaped by *dukkha*, and our response is infused with desire. Desire is the crucible within which the self is formed. This is why it was so important to Freud and why it remains the essential kernel of psychotherapy. If we are out of touch with our desires, we cannot be ourselves. In this way of thinking, desire is our vitality, an essential component of our human experience, that which gives us our individuality and at the same time keeps prodding us out of ourselves. Desire is a longing for completion in the face of the vast unpredictability of our predicament. It is "the natural," and if it is chased away it returns with a vengeance.

In the Sufi tradition that Nasruddin exemplifies, human yearning is understood to be a reflection of God's desire to be known. To the Sufi, God is hidden, but wishes to be found. The clue to God's presence lies in the depth of our longing. Only by dwelling in the insatiable, and infinite, quality of desire can the Sufi begin to appreciate God's nature. While I have been much more drawn to the non-theistic tradition of Buddhism, where the notion of God is deemed irrelevant to a person's spiritual strivings, the Sufi perspective on longing is not far removed from the left-handed path. The infinite can be known through an acceptance of, and opening to, the unending quality of yearning. My interest in writing this book, in fact, is to correct

the still-dominant misperception that Buddhism strives to eliminate desire.

The actual word that the Buddha used to describe the cause
of *dukkha* was not desire, it was *tanha*, which means "thirst," or
"craving." It connotes what we might also call clinging: the attempt to hold on to an ungraspable experience, not the desire
for happiness or completion. As a therapist who has spent the
past thirty years engaged in an integration of Buddhism with
psychotherapy, I have seen how crucial this distinction can be.
To set desire up as the enemy and then try to eliminate it is to
seek to destroy one of our most precious human qualities, our
natural response to the truth of suffering. Buddhism was not
intended to be a path of destruction, it was a path of self-
understanding. It did not seek to divide and conquer, it sought
wholeness and integration. Hidden within its vast panoply of
teachings, in fact, was a way of working with desire that completely contradicts the usual interpretation of Buddhism as
encouraging renunciation and detachment. These teachings
about the enlightening potential of desire were traditionally
kept secret, because of their tendency to be misunderstood and
abused, yet without them, the full value of the Buddhist approach cannot be appreciated.

In its path of desire, Buddhism has a natural counterpart in
contemporary psychoanalysis. Both traditions encourage an appreciation of the important links between the spiritual and the
sensual: the ways in which erotic experience can be transcendent and spiritual experiences erotic. In a metaphor that Freud
would undoubtedly have approved of, the Tibetan Buddhist
model for the awakened mind is orgasm, because it is only at
the climax of lovemaking (in worldly life) that the veils of ignorance drop away. There is an understanding in both traditions of

the multidimensional levels of what we call the self, the ways in which we can be seeking comfort, closeness, pleasure, affirmation, release and oblivion all at the same time, from the same persons, places or things.

AWAKENING TO DESIRE

What distinguishes the *tantric*, or left-handed, path is its recognition that desire itself can be transformed through a process that is at once mental, emotional, psychological and spiritual. This is a path that involves not so much *physical* exercise as *mental* exercise, a gradual change in the way we relate to desire, in which longing becomes a teacher in its own right. The key to this path is to make desire into a meditation. This idea strikes many as anathema. It is much easier to set desire up as the enemy and isolate it from everything else that we value. When it is split off or demonized it can still be enjoyed guiltily but it never has to be integrated with our loftier impulses. We can continue to look down on desire, or on those who are desiring, when we are not in the grip of it ourselves, and thereby preserve some spurious notion of superiority. As Freud suggested many years ago, there is something vaguely disgusting about desire, something that might have its origins in a repugnance that many feel toward the genitals. "All neurotics," Freud noted, with his characteristic deadpan humor, "and many others besides, take exception to the fact that *inter urinas et faeces nascimur* (we are born between urine and feces).'"[4]

It is this shame or reticence toward desire that has marked most of the spiritual traditions of both East and West. To paraphrase Nietzsche, who described the Christian attack on erotic desire, Christianity didn't kill eros, it just made it vicious. From the Puritanism of American culture to the Eastern view that the seeds of suffering lie in the endless pursuit of passion, much of the world is deeply conflicted about a trait that virtually all people share. Yet for me, this divisive approach is no longer tenable. The separation of the spiritual from the sensual, of the sacred from the relational, and of the enlightened from the erotic no longer seems desirable. Certainly, seeing how impossible the division has proven for the countless spiritual teachers of every tradition who have stumbled over their own longings has been instructive. In addition, having a family and a relationship has made it abundantly clear to me that they require the same dedication, passion and vision that a spiritual journey demands. Now that spiritual life is in the hands of householders rather than monastics, the demands of desire are front and center, not hidden from view.

Desire is one of the most misunderstood concepts in Western spiritual circles. In groups that come together to learn more about meditation or yoga, it is a question that is almost always at the top of the agenda. The notion of detachment, which is fundamental to an Eastern approach to life, now seems more problematic than it used to, given the need that most people feel for intimacy. The Buddha left his wife and young child, after all, to begin his spiritual search. Is this the model we are trying to live up to in our relationships?

At a recent conference in New York City, for example, someone asked the writer and Buddhist scholar Stephen Batchelor about this issue:

"I have no trouble understanding the idea of non-attachment in meditation," the questioner said, "but when it comes to my marriage and family, I don't get it. Why is non-attachment even a positive thing to aspire to?" Attachment, even desire, seemed to the questioner like something to be supported in the interpersonal realm, not something to be overcome.

Stephen motioned to his wife, Martine, who was just coming into the room. "My wife says it is like holding a coin," he said, and he held out one arm with his palm up and his fist closed. "We can hold it like this," and he emphasized the closed nature of his fist, "or we can hold it like this," and he opened his hand to show the coin sitting in the center of his palm. "The closed fist is like clinging," he said. "But with my hand open, I still hold the coin." Buddhism, Stephen seemed to be implying, actually imagines that desire can be held lightly. The distinction between the closed and the open fist is the distinction between clinging and desire. Although the Buddha saw the cause of suffering in craving, he did not say that the cure was to simply eliminate desire. His "direct" path was actually much more circuitous.

Before his enlightenment, the almost-Buddha actually did try to eliminate desire from his being. This was the more obvious approach to the problem of desire and was already well established in his time. India, even then, was a land of renunciates. In accordance with the spiritual practices of his day, the future Buddha engaged in all sorts of austerities designed to rid his soul of longing. He sat on a stone seat, fasted and punished himself in every imaginable way; there are famous sculptures from what is now Afghanistan showing his emaciated body with his ribs jutting out from so much penance. His asceticism was said to have no match in ancient India.

But the Buddha found that he would kill himself with such practices before achieving any kind of lasting peace of mind. In taking his penance to its logical extreme, the Buddha realized that the world would not tolerate his elimination of eros. It would eliminate him instead. He concluded that there had to be another way and went on to evolve the route between austerities and sensory indulgence that became known as the Middle Path. This is a tricky place to dwell, a between space, that Stephen was also pointing to in his example of the open palm. It is a space where desire is not pushed away but where its inevitable failures are also tolerated, where we open to it just as it is. In this place, one does not reject pleasure but one is not dependent on it either. Desire is given room to breathe while the desirer is urged to examine its qualities. "Look into the nature of desire," counseled the great Tibetan yogi Padmasambhava, "and there is boundless light."[5]

THE PATH OF DESIRE

The Buddha's path did not focus on desire as an enemy to be conquered but rather as an energy to be perceived correctly. The Buddha was interested in teaching us not only how to find our own freedom, but in how to stay in affectionate relationship to other people. While he counseled his followers to be lights unto themselves, he also recognized how much we need each other to make freedom possible. There is as much emphasis on compassion in the Buddha's teachings as there is on wisdom, and it is clear that one route to the development of such compassion is through the investigation, not elimination, of one's own desire.

In this approach is a very sophisticated psychological path, one that is mirrored and supported by our own tradition of psychoanalytic psychotherapy, also devoted to the intensive study of desire. These are the two traditions that have most influenced my own work as a therapist, and it is their accumulated wisdom with regard to desire that I wish to explore in this book. It is a task that I could never have undertaken, however, if I had not been exposed, early in my career, to the psychological wisdom contained in the ancient traditions of India.

The Indian subcontinent, while as ambivalent about desire as everywhere else in the world, is nevertheless filled with a reverence for the enlightening potential of eros and the tenderness of the human heart. It is a land profoundly influenced by an ancient appreciation of desire, one where this openness has shaped the culture. From its sacred cows, symbol of the Mother, whose milk and dung provide nourishment, fuel and shelter, to its sacred temples adorned with symbols and scenes of divine eroticism, India is suffused with the colors, smells, fabrics, flavors and faces of devotion. Its monuments, even those dating back two thousand years to the first flourishing of the Buddha's teachings, are architectural representations of the transformation of desire; and its myths, Hindu epics like the endlessly repeated love and adventure story the *Ramayana*, which figures so prominently in this book, teach its listeners how to turn their own love relationships into aspects of the divine. India is rich in the natural resources of human emotion and it holds a model for desire that is much more integrated than our own.

In my introduction to India, I was offered a peek into a culture steeped in the path of desire, one in which pleasure is the image of the divine state: where it *is* the ladder, not just a rung reaching toward the heavens. In a certain way, the Indian approach is a reflection of the Freudian one. For Freud, everything was sexual, even desire for God. In his famous comments about religious experience, which he called the oceanic feeling, he reduced the oneness that is knowable through mystical insight to the erotic experience of the infant at the mother's breast. In much of Indian thought, however, everything is spiritual, even the desire for sex. The most sacred temples are built on a model of deified eroticism.

My own view is that both are true. Each dimension mirrors the other. Freud understood that our erotic lives contain a distilled, essential, stripped-down version of the enormity of our psyches, while the Indian traditions recognized that attention to the erotic landscape opens up transcendent understanding. As Freud once admitted in a conversation with a prominent existential psychiatrist: Everything is instinct, but everything is also spirit.[6]

In this work, I have focused on Hindu myths, Buddhist teachings and psychoanalytic theory. In my discussions of worldly desire, I have concentrated primarily on intimate life and sexual yearnings. In keeping with Freud's discoveries and with my own training as a psychotherapist, I have found that an unabashed observation of intimate life permits a clear perception of otherwise hidden dynamics of the psyche. This is not to suggest that desire is only sexual, but that within sexuality we can find a model for much of human experience. Within the psychotherapy world, this reduction of things to their sexual bedrock has, in fact, moved somewhat out of fashion. As the schools of what have become known as object relations and relational psychotherapy have grown in popularity, there has been a profound recognition that individuals are seeking relationships and affirmation as much as sexual discharge or erotic release. Yet I have chosen to remember the erotic underpinnings of human psychological experience and to focus on them whenever possible; not to exclude the relational and spiritual but to show how all three: the sexual, the interpersonal and the spiritual, exist on one continuum and are part and parcel of one another. As we open to desire, things do not become less sexual, they become more erotic. Desire seeks wholeness and desire seeks bliss—and it can find them in unusual places. My endeavor in this work is to keep intimate life in focus, using it as a template for an exploration of what is essential, and spiritual, about desire. I want to try to keep the baby from being thrown out with the bathwater.

I have divided this book into four sections, based on the Buddha's Four Noble Truths, charting the path that desire can take us on if we are able to use it for spiritual growth. Each section begins with a quotation from a famous Hindu epic called the *Ramayana*, a story of thwarted love between a man and a woman who, unbeknownst to them, are also incarnations of God. The *Ramayana* charts the same course that my four sections describe: a progression, driven by desire, from incompleteness to wholeness, a metaphorical depiction of the path of desire.

The first section, For Want of Desire, is based on the way things usually are. We think that we exist apart from the rest of the world. Our desires are urgent and conditioned by duality. We feel incomplete and are aware of our own flaws and imperfections. Love relations, and desire in general, are driven by objectification, not by openness. We feel "in need" and the "object" of our affection has to gratify us. It never quite does the trick and we have to deal with the gap between self and other, the gap that desire cannot bridge. We think we know all about desire, but, in fact, we are not open to it at all.

The second section, Clinging, describes what happens when

we start to realize that there is no such thing as an ultimately satisfying object. This is where the first confrontations with clinging take place, since the obstacles to our growth, called *fixations* in Buddhism, originate in the effort to find an ultimately satisfying object. In this phase of spiritual development, a certain kind of renunciation is necessary, in order to differentiate craving or "thirst" from desire.

In the third section, The End of Clinging, comes the flowering of subjective life. When desire is not denied or suppressed, but instead allowed to grow in the light of there being no ultimately satisfying self or object, a tremendous development of inner life is possible. The finding of a third way with desire, not denying and not grasping, is what the Buddha's psychology makes possible. Out of this new approach comes the ability to empathize with another's personal experience. No longer relating to others as "objects" that exist solely to gratify or deny us, a person in this phase is able to transform his or her intimate experiences into spiritual nourishment.

The fourth and final section, A Path for Desire, describes the essential principles that allow us to get the most out of desire, to use it rather than being used by it. When desire is no longer used to attack a world that is perceived as separate but instead immerses us fully in the pleasures that surround us, a new kind of satisfaction is possible. At that point, even the bathwater has potential.

· I ·

FOR WANT
OF DESIRE

Ravana looked at Sita and he thought—Mine.

Ramayana *(p. 176)*

1

Ramayana

The grandest and most vivid portrayal in all of Indian mythology—indeed, in all of the world's mythologies— of the enlightening potential of desire can be found in an ancient Hindu epic, the *Ramayana*. One of India's most popular tales, the *Ramayana*, 25,000 verses long, is a story about the movement from clinging to pure desire. While it is a Hindu tale, it embodies a universal wisdom, one that is also vividly portrayed in the Buddhist path of desire. The *Ramayana* describes, in mythic form, the journey that is possible from clinging to non-clinging when desire is acknowledged as a path in its own right. Its main characters, the lovers Sita and Rama, are buffeted back and forth between union and separation throughout the tale, aided in their attempts to reunite by a famous monkey named Hanuman. Like the Buddha's teachings, the *Ramayana*, written sometime between 220 B.C. and 200 A.D., was carried all over Asia, only recently reaching the West. Its stories adorn the walls of Buddhist temple complexes at Angkor Wat in Cambodia, built one thousand years later, and it is still performed in predominantly Muslim Indonesia, where its vitality has survived long after the decline of both the Buddhist and Hindu religions. While it is a Hindu tale, its lessons have been embraced by peoples of many different religions.

I read the *Ramayana* for the first time on my honeymoon in Bali and Java and was amazed to see its stories acted out in dance, puppet shows and theater while I was grappling, in my own internal way, with the implications of the story for my marriage. It seemed as if, during my month's immersion in the tale, I was living it, reading it and seeing it everywhere. When my wife and I had children, the *Ramayana* was one of the first long stories that we read to them. When my daughter, at around age four, first entered a synagogue, she whispered to me, as she gazed at the tabernacle where the Torah is stored, "Is that where Hanuman lives?" The universality of the story was not lost on her either.

While the love that connects Sita and Rama is never in doubt throughout the long separation that defines most of the story, it is their desire for each other that keeps them seeking reunion. One way of reading the *Ramayana* is as a teaching in how to use desire in the service of love: how to use the inevitable expanse that one finds between lover and beloved as a vehicle for greater wisdom and compassion. While the imaginative structure of the *Ramayana* is completely different from a modern psychodynamic text, its message is one that can be easily translated into the psychological language of our time: The gap between lover and beloved is the space where the most critical emotional and spiritual work takes place.

This is not the conventional interpretation of the story, of course, one of the most popular in all of South and Southeast Asia. For some, it is merely a fantastic adventure story, the tale of a huge battle between the exiled prince Rama and his army of animal helpers on one side; and the demon king Ravana and his force of unrepentant *rakshasas*, a race of powerful beings living on the island of Lanka who have managed to kidnap Rama's lovely wife, Sita. For some it is primarily a story of devotion centering on the monkey-god Hanuman, who is something of a trickster but who is completely at the service of Rama, saving his life and rescuing his wife from the evil demons. For others, it is a divine romance, a tale of undying love between Sita and Rama, two aspects of one divinity whose separation from each other is purely illusion, acted out for the benefit of their devotees.

While lessons about desire are indeed present in the story, they are not what is commonly attended to, at least not consciously. Sita and Rama are certainly lovers, but Rama (unbeknownst to him) is an incarnation of Vishnu, an aspect of God. It is standard practice, in fact, to see all of the passion in the story as an allegory for the love of God. It is easy, under the spell of the divine, to ignore the teachings about human desire that are implicit in the tale. My old friend and teacher Ram Dass (whose own Hindu name means, "servant of Rama") virtually scoffed at my interpretation when I presented it to him.

"Rama and Sita are pure people," he reminded me. "Human desire goes in a different category. The ego has many desires; the only desire the soul has is to merge with God."

While there is truth to what Ram Dass told me, I do not entirely agree with him, at least as far as accepting the strict division between what the soul wants and what the ego wants. This splitting apart of the self into lower and higher is one of the unskillful tendencies that the *Ramayana* story addresses. While it is inevitable to some degree for desire to go astray, the denigration of desire can itself become one of the ways that its wisdom is thwarted. To see desire as limited to the realm of the ego and therefore always potentially dangerous is to miss its true nature. Ultimately, the power of desire can be harnessed for spiritual growth. This is the message of the *Ramayana*.

There is an amusing story from the Zen Buddhist tradition of Japan about a Zen monk scrawling a poem across the face of an erotic painting of a courtesan. He wrote the following:

Up and down,
Up and down,
I've got a lot of
Endurance—
Doesn't anyone notice my true purpose?[1]

The *Ramayana* is the story of desire's discovery of its true purpose: the overcoming of the clinging or craving that the Buddha described as the origin of suffering. What is remarkable about it is that this overcoming of clinging is accomplished in the context of an ever-deepening and intensifying passion. While the tendency of desire to fragment, to split itself into lower and higher, instinctual and spiritual, or human and divine, is the subtext of the tale, desire's ability to resolve these splits is the story's essence. In the *Ramayana*, this split and its resolution are acted out literally. Part of the reason for the tale's longevity and popularity, I believe, is that the difficulties faced by its protagonists are our difficulties also. Like Sita and Rama, we all have to learn how to navigate the waters of our most intimate relationships, face the loneliness and separateness that come with love, and confront the demons that keep us from knowing the divinity of our desire.

THE STORY

The *Ramayana* begins with a fierce battle between gods and demons. Much of heaven is laid waste and the demon king, Ravana, extracts a boon from Brahma, the highest of the gods, that he shall be unslayable by every creature of Heaven and of the underworlds. But Ravana, like the human ego he comes to represent, is careless and proud. He neglects to request protection from humans and animals, not thinking that they could ever be a threat. In recognition of his oversight, the great gods Vishnu and Lakshmi are propitiated by the other gods into taking human birth. Vishnu splits himself into four parts and incarnates as four brothers, with Prince Rama of Ayodhya the eldest and strongest. The goddess Lakshmi incarnates as Sita, fated to be Rama's wife. In their human forms, Rama and Sita have no consciousness of their divinity, but they are nevertheless virtuous and honorable as would befit their heavenly lineage. Rama is groomed to take over the kingdom of his father but after the treachery of his stepmother is persuaded to abdicate the throne in favor of his half-brother while accepting a thirteen-year banishment to the forest accompanied by Sita and another half-brother, Lakshmana.

In India, the forest is the equivalent of the unconscious. It is the place outside of the rules and regulations of the home where spiritual seekers have always taken refuge. In the Buddha's story, the forest is where he goes to search for truth after discovering the reality of impermanence and suffering. In the *Ramayana*, the forest is a place of magic and mystery, populated by all the hybrid characters of Indian mythology. It is in the forest that the fated confrontation between Ravana and Rama unfolds.

It is Ravana's desire that brings him into Rama's orbit and Sita's desire that leads her astray. Ravana spies Sita and is smitten by her. He convinces a wizard friend to change him into an enchanted deer to capture Sita's attention when she is alone at her campsite, waiting for Rama and Lakshmana to return. Against her own better judgment, she follows the deer, and soon she is spirited away in Ravana's golden chariot, south to Lanka, land of the demons. The splitting of conventional desire is established by this kidnapping. Ravana is the king of ego and sensual longing, but Sita, after the deception of the deer is revealed, remains focused on Rama. As if to demonstrate this, at the moment of her abduction she drops her jewels into the waiting arms of two onlooking monkeys, pivotal characters who later in the story assist Rama and serve as his emissaries. The description in the story, which was meant to be sung in the Sanskrit verses of the original, is very beautiful:

> Sita reached down her hands and broke the anklets off from her legs and let them fall down on that plain-looking hill. She took off her earrings and dropped them. Sita let all the ornaments of Anasuya fall, and she tied Guha's necklace in her yellow scarf edged with gold and dropped it also. Ravana did not

notice. He sped away, and Sita's hair streamed out on the wind, and they left behind the two monkeys.

The two monkeys watched with their yellow-brown eyes never blinking, while Sita's gold and silver bells and bracelets fell ringing down and crying. The yellow scarf flashed down like lightning; the silver ornaments were the Moon and white stars dropping.[2]

Sita is suddenly and precipitously reduced to the common human predicament: She is cut off from God and is at the mercy of ignorance and instinct. The thing that makes her, in Ram Dass's words, "pure," is that she remembers her beloved and resists the co-opting of her desire. Sita is not desireless and not asexual, but her desire, after the brief interlude with the deer, is entirely focused on Rama. Although she is tortured by the multiheaded Ravana, emblem of addictive desire, she has no difficulty resisting his utter objectification of her. While Ravana's desire is to possess her completely, he is endlessly rebuffed in his quest. Sita cannot be swayed, although her faith in Rama is not as unwavering as her repulsion of his enemy.

While it is easy to scoff at Ravana's hubris, it would be a mistake to dismiss him too easily. He is not an unsympathetic character. He may be a demon, but in his entreaties to Sita, he can sound remarkably human. Ravana is us, trying to possess the objects of our affection, trying to merge with an objectified and idealized beloved. In his belief in the power of "objects" to satisfy his hunger, he exemplifies the clinging of the Second Noble Truth. He does everything he can to earn Sita's affection. He reminds me of a patient of mine: a big, likeable, energetic, extremely intelligent and sensitive man who often complained that his wife refused to have enough sex with him.

"I pay lots of attention to getting her aroused, to getting her off," he would tell me, as if I thought he was selfish. "Why doesn't she want it as much as I do?" He could hardly wait for his children to go to sleep so that they could "get randy," but she would all too often tell him politely that she was not in the mood.

"What *is* arousing for her?" I asked him one afternoon, and he became suddenly morose. He scanned his memory for a long time in silence. Then he remembered something that had happened not so long ago. His wife had asked him to help move some boxes that were cluttering up their front hall. If he would move the boxes, she had said, she would be more in the mood. He had been dismissive of her hint; it had not made any sense to him. Yet that was the only clue that came to mind. The story was all the more poignant because of the association that followed:

"My own father never did anything nice for my mother," my patient softly recounted. "But he would come up to her from behind and grope her breasts in front of us."

My patient was like Ravana when he had trouble empathizing with his wife's point of view, when he wanted simply to possess her without taking her desire into account. His failure to have his way with her, however, opened up the possibility, in my office, of newly appreciating her separateness and accepting his own. This was the key to a deeper connection. It was strange to him that the boxes in the hall could have anything to do with their sexual relationship, but this acknowledgment was the prerequisite for a rekindling of desire in their relationship. The *Ramayana* tells a similar story. Sita and Rama have to find their way back to each other once they are established as separate persons, divided by an ocean and under the siege of the demons. They may be divine, but on earth they have to act out the human predicament.

Rama, incarnation of Vishnu, unsuspecting manifestation of God, is bereft when Sita is taken away. Cut off from her, he seeks help from the monkey Hanuman and a host of other animals. Hanuman, the embodiment of devotion, brings Sita's jewels to Rama and then takes a gold ring back to her as a symbol of Rama's unflagging love, a ring given to him by Sita's father at the time of their marriage. Sita welcomes Hanuman, takes the ring and gives him one more jewel, a pearl mounted on a gold leaf that her father had tied into her hair on the day of her wedding. She refuses Hanuman's offer to fly her back to Rama, insisting that he come to free her himself. Sita demands nothing less than complete reunion, even if it takes an epic battle to accomplish it.

SON OF THE WIND

Rama is able to free Sita only by securing the help of Hanuman. Hanuman, the monkey-god, son of the wind, is the bridge between the two lovers, the vehicle that helps them overcome the obstacle of possessive ego that has come between them. Both the wind and the monkey, in Indian thought, stand for the mind. As the son of the wind, Hanuman's crucial role in the story suggests how important the training of the mind is for overcoming the gap that desire leaves in its wake. Hanuman's role is to bridge the gap that ego creates: to break down the tendency to objectify the beloved and open up an appreciation of the subjective, and ungraspable, aspect of another's experience.

Hanuman taps the creative potential of the human imagination. He fills the intermediate space between lover and beloved, the space that must be trained in meditation in order that desire not fall victim to frustration and disappointment. Hanuman represents the inner life that the confrontation with *dukkha* opens up. But his job is to help differentiate pure desire from the clinging that tends to obscure it.

Hanuman's exploits fill the central part of the *Ramayana*. It is he who discovers where Sita is being held captive and he who journeys to furtively meet with her. In one famous leap, he straddles the ocean between India and Lanka, and after confronting Ravana he sets the entire city on fire with his burning tail. Returning to Rama, he recruits an army of talking animals to build a massive bridge across the ocean to set the scene for the final climactic battle in which Rama can finally rescue Sita and bring her home. It is only at this point that Rama discovers his divine origins.

In the *Ramayana*, Sita and Rama's physical separation is a metaphor for the separation of subject and object or lover and beloved. Sita's rescue depends on a third force that can bridge the distance between them. Embodied by the monkey Hanuman, son of the wind, this liminal character is the key to the resolution of one of desire's most persistent dilemmas. For in a certain way, desire does not know quite what to do with itself. It seeks union, possession or complete satisfaction, but never completely achieves it. As the Buddha recognized in his First Noble Truth and as Freud agreed many centuries later, there is a residual dissatisfaction in even the most satisfying experience. The object always disappoints.

Hanuman's character demonstrates the way through this

problem, the most crucial aspect of the path of desire. In creating a bridge to Lanka, helped by an animal army recruited to the cause of reuniting the separated lovers, Hanuman shows that it is possible to break down the tendency to objectify both the self and the beloved. In confronting the tendency toward objectification, Hanuman and his helpers function the way the *transitional object* aids a young child in a psychodynamic model: A bridge between self and other is created that makes an appreciation of their fluid natures possible. For instance, when a young child plays imaginatively with a favorite stuffed animal, one of the things that happens is that his or her inner life is deepened. The "transitional" function of this play is to help the child tolerate a separateness that would otherwise feel overwhelming. Play helps a child not take separation too seriously. In helping Sita and Rama reunite, Hanuman shows them how deepening their intimacy depends on how they understand the gap between them.[3]

Desire is central to the story of Rama and Sita. It rips them apart but ultimately brings them together again. As symbolized by their jewels, which they pass back and forth through the intermediary of the monkey, their desire eventually fuels their reunion. When Sita casts her ornaments down, she lights up the sky with her desire. Like shooting stars, they burn brightly and then fall into the care of the monkeys, pivotal characters who symbolize the ability to harness desire's fiery energy. Part of Sita and Rama's spiritual work is to figure out what to do with their desire: how to manage it and how to use it in the service of their love. Their struggle is our struggle. How can we prevent desire from being hijacked by the divisive force of clinging? How can we use desire to help us know the divine?

SOMETHING LACKING

Desire can be a stubborn problem, one that can seem interminable. At the very close of Freud's life, in one of his final notes found scrawled on a single page of paper, we can see him still wrestling with his version of the problem:

> *The ultimate ground of all intellectual inhibitions and all inhibitions of work seems to be the inhibition of masturbation in childhood. But perhaps it goes deeper; perhaps it is not inhibition by external influences but its unsatisfying nature in itself. There is always something lacking for complete discharge and satisfaction—en attendant toujours quelquechose qui ne venait point. . . .* [4]

Freud's French phrase is his definition of desire: *"always waiting for something which never came."* In this phrase, Freud rubs up directly against the First Noble Truth of discontent while unknowingly referencing Sita's plight in Lanka. Nothing seems quite right. Even pleasure disappoints. There is always a residual sense of something lacking. But the *Ramayana* affirms something else, just as the Buddha did. While one aspect of desire's nature is certainly the gap between satisfaction and fulfillment, desire's ultimate goal is to free us from clinging. Sita's lover *does* come to her. To counter Freud's pessimism, we must travel the path outlined by the *Ramayana*. It is our own clinging, the cause of this "something lacking," that the yoga of desire seeks to help us with.

Desire, in its most fundamental form, recognizes the sense of incompleteness that is endemic to the human condition. It seeks a freedom from this incompleteness in any form it can imagine: physical, sensual, emotional, intellectual or spiritual. But like Sita entranced by the golden deer, we chase phenomena we can never truly possess. Yet as Sita learned through her various misfortunes, desire can be freed from the tendency to cling. As this happens, the sense of "self" and "other" becomes transformed as well.

These are the discoveries that Sita makes, imprisoned in the *sinsapa* grove by the demon king, wondering if her lover has forsaken her. First, Hanuman comes to her, bringing with him the promise of a bridge to her own separateness. Then, Rama arrives. A new kind of union becomes possible: one in which she becomes more than the object of another's desire; where her own voice, separate though it may be, is answered. Only then can her true oneness with Rama be appreciated.

As the *Ramayana* makes clear, desire has a vision that is paradoxical, a vision that can both confuse and enlighten us. It can make us feel ourselves and lose ourselves at the same time. We can be as pure as Sita, as demonic as Ravana, as devoted as Hanuman, or as skeptical as Freud. Whatever our stance, we cannot escape its importance in our lives. Perhaps this is why the Buddha was careful to hold desire so lightly in his teachings. For desire, in its paradoxical nature, in its ability to simultaneously breach and maintain the space between lovers, in the way it both connects and separates, and in the manner in which it forces us to reconcile love and hate, is often as close as we come to liberation in our regular lives. Like the animal-headed goddesses who guard the entrances to some ancient Indian temples, desire summons, ties, binds and maddens, even as it ushers us toward innermost bliss.[5] It is desire, after all, that makes us seek liberation in the first place.

2

The Left-Handed Path

There is a story in the annals of Zen that speaks to the unusual delicacy with which desire is held in the Buddhist tradition. It is the foundation story of Zen, the seed story, the tale that is told about the origin of the tradition, and the fragment that contains the essence of the whole. As in most such stories, at least in the Zen tradition, almost nothing happens. In this case, we could say that only two small things happened. The first was that the Buddha, during a sermon at a spot called Vulture's Peak, held up a flower. Some accounts of the event specify that the flower that he held up was a golden lotus. Most of the monks in the grand assembly did not know what to make of this sermon. There was nothing else to it. Just a flower.

It must have been similar to the time that the composer John Cage was invited to give a performance to an American

Buddhist audience at the newly formed Naropa Institute in Boulder, Colorado. He did something related: He gave a concert that was mostly silence with only the vaguest projections of randomly created drawings illuminating the stage behind him. The Buddhist audience grew irate but the Tibetan founder of the institute called Cage the next day to offer him a job teaching at the university.

There is no record of the community at Vulture's Peak growing irate, but it is said that everyone in the audience, except for one seasoned monk, was puzzled. Only a man named Kasyapa, sometimes known as Mahakasyapa (the *great* Kasyapa), understood. Kasyapa smiled. This was the second thing that happened: Kasyapa smiled. The Buddha, seeing that he understood, responded (in some accounts) with the following words, "I possess the True Dharma Eye, the Marvelous Mind of Nirvana. I entrust it to Mahakasyapa."[1]

The story is used, in Zen Buddhism, to illustrate the power of what is called "mind-to-mind transmission," the passing of the Buddha's understanding, outside of the vocabulary of words or letters, from master to master in an unbroken chain down to the present. To the extent that anyone tries to explain what the Buddha was illustrating with the flower, it is usually thought to be the ineffable experience of "thusness," the fact that the world, and our minds, just *are*, in the same way the flower in the Buddha's hand just *is*. Some also note that the lotus is an ancient symbol in the Buddhist world for the enlightened mind. Just as the lotus grows out of the muck of the pond without having to send down roots into the earth, so does nirvana grow from the muck of the mind without our having to dig down to the roots of our neuroses. Enlightenment, like the lotus, blooms spontaneously if conditions are right.

But it is possible that there was another meaning to the Buddha's gesture, not one that contradicts any of the above, but one that was a bit more to the point. This alternative interpretation is not the classic one, and it is not one that I have ever heard from anyone else. But to me, in thinking about questions of desire, it makes a lot of sense.

In Indian mythology, the flower is quite a specific symbol. When the Buddha, years before his sermon on Vulture's Peak, was seeking his own enlightenment, it is said that a character named Mara the Tempter repeatedly attacked and tested him with his arrows of desire. But the Buddha, through the power of his understanding, turned the rain of Mara's arrows into a cascade of flowers that showered down over him harmlessly. Shafts of desire become flowers when confronted by a Buddha. The personification of eros in India, the Indian Cupid, is a god named Kama (for whom the *Kama Sutra* is felicitously named) whose magical bow has a string of buzzing bees, and whose five arrows are also made of flowers, sharpened, it is said, by longing. The bees and the flowers give a sense of desire's double-edged nature, its capacity to both tease and delight, frustrate and fulfill. Kama's nickname, Madana, means the "Intoxicator."[2] And throughout Asian history, the lotus, in particular, has always represented female sexuality,[3] due to its obvious resemblance to the female genitalia. Indeed, the very word that was used to address the Buddha, the honorific Sanskrit title *Bhagwan*, has its derivation in the word for vulva.

Thus, the Buddha's decision to hold up a flower could very easily have had a not-so-secret meaning. The connotation of desire would inevitably have passed through his devotees' minds. Most of them clearly did not know what to make of the Buddha's gesture. What could he be indicating about flowers, or about desire, or about silence? They held their attention steadfast, as, undoubtedly, they had been trained to do. The surprising thing is that one of the monks responded at all.

Desire was an important issue in the Buddha's time, just as it is in ours. The Buddha emerged in an era dominated by a struggle between materialism and asceticism. There was great wealth in the princely courts and in the newly emerging merchant classes, great opportunity for sensory indulgence of all kinds. And there was a strong forest tradition of renunciation, naked yogis smearing themselves with ashes and performing all kinds of austerities, most of which the Buddha had once practiced to an extreme. So desire, on either side, was fraught. Much as in our time, there seemed to be only two choices: Surrender to desire or try to get rid of it completely.

When Kasyapa smiled, he was indicating that he understood something very important. The flower itself was the teaching. Desire was okay. It could be held by the Buddha's teachings and infused with the stillness of the Buddha's mind. It, too, had Buddha nature. And, not unrelatedly, smiling was the appropriate response. The Buddha's teachings were remarkable because they made room for a smile about desire.

THE MIDDLE WAY

When the Buddha gave his very first sermon, after walking a fair distance from the site of his enlightenment to the area of modern-day Sarnath in the Gangetic plain of Northern India, he also spoke of desire. His teaching from that time is known by its Sanskrit name, translated as "Setting Rolling the Wheel of the *Dharma.*" The word *"dharma,"* which has been rendered in English variously as "the truth," "the way" or "the law," is virtually untranslatable. Yet it is the dharma that encapsulates all the Buddha's psychological and spiritual teachings. The root of the word *dher* means to hold firmly or to support. This root can be found in the English word throne, from the Greek *dhrono* or *thronos,* and in the Latin-derived words firm, firmament and infirmary. The wheel of the dharma holds something, as the firmament holds the stars, as a throne holds a king, as the infirmary holds people who are suffering and as a vase, spun on a potter's wheel, holds emptiness. The wheel of the dharma, the Buddha indicated as he spoke, holds desire.

In setting the wheel rolling, the Buddha gave the first exposition of the Middle Path. He unleashed a new vision, and he hoped, by the power of his words, to set this *chakra,* or wheel, turning in the minds of those who listened to him teach. It was a new beginning, and it involved a new yoga, a new way of holding desire.

> *Bhikkhus, there are these two extremes that ought not to be cultivated by one who has gone forth. What two? There is devotion to pursuit of pleasure in sensual desires, which is low, coarse, vulgar, ignoble and harmful; and there is devotion to self-mortification, which is painful, ignoble and harmful. The middle way discovered by the Perfect One avoids both these extremes; it gives vision, gives knowledge, and leads to peace, to direct knowledge, to enlightenment, to Nirvana.*[4]

In setting up a Middle Way that fell between the two extremes of sensory indulgence and renunciation, the Buddha left plenty of room for an exploration of desire. His teachings on the subject can be roughly divided into two categories: the right-handed path of renunciation and monasticism in which sensory desires are avoided and the left-handed path of passion and relationship in which sensory desires are not avoided but are made into objects of meditation. This latter path—the left-handed one—is traditionally the one that is kept secret and hidden. Its points are thought to be too open to misinterpretation and confusion to be talked about directly, and a secret language, like that of the flower and the smile, had to be developed to communicate its insights. While his early exhortations encouraged his disciples to follow in his footsteps and renounce the householder life, as the Buddha's teachings spread and took root, their relevance, even for the everyday life of passion and relationship, began to be revealed. It is in this context that the Buddha's flower sermon, understood by the great Kasyapa, is especially relevant.

In that first sermon setting the wheel of the dharma rolling, the Buddha expounded his formulation of the Four Noble Truths, the central psychology of what has come to be known as Buddhism and the central teaching of both the right-handed and the left-handed approach. As we have seen, his First Noble Truth is that all of life is tinged with a sense of pervasive unsatisfactoriness because of how fleeting and insubstantial everything is. His Second Noble Truth is that the cause of this discontent is clinging, "thirst" or craving. His Third Noble Truth proclaims the possibility of an end to the problem, and his Fourth Noble Truth explains the Eightfold Path of mental, ethical and relational training that can bring this about: the so-called Middle Path. The central role of desire in this formulation is clear, but, as I have already indicated, it is often misinterpreted.

What the Buddha *actually* suggested is that it is the *avoidance* of the elusiveness of the object of desire that is the origin of suffering. The problem is not desire: it is clinging to, or craving, a particular outcome, one in which there is no remainder, in which the object is completely under our power. As my Buddhist teacher, Joseph Goldstein, always makes clear, as an object of desire, that which we long for causes suffering, but as an object of mindfulness it can lead to awakening. The trick, as far as Buddhism is concerned, is to accept the fact that no experience can ever be as complete as we would wish, that no object can ever satisfy completely. In the right-handed path, the Buddha's followers turned away from the pursuit of sensory pleasure, but in the left-handed path, they allowed themselves to come face-to-face with the gap that desire always comes up against, as well as any pleasure that it might bring.

Allowing ourselves into desire's abyss turns out to be the key to a more complete enjoyment of its fruits. By experiencing desire in its totality: gratifying and frustrating, sweet and bitter, pleasant and painful, successful and yet coming up short, we can use it to awaken our minds. The dualities that desire seems to take for granted can be resolved through a willingness to drop into the gap between them. Even living in the world of the senses, we can be free. To my mind, this was the secret message of the Buddha's nonverbal exchange with Kasyapa.

EROTIC LONGING

In my own experience, I can see that I was drawn to meditation out of a certain kind of erotic longing. The sensual and the spiritual were mixed up with each other right from the start, so it was perhaps natural that I would be drawn to the left-handed teachings. It was perplexing to me at the time; I did not really know what I was looking for or why I was looking for it or even what force was propelling me to keep looking, but I kept finding myself, in my early twenties, circling particular kinds of information that had to do with Eastern spiritual practices, in the same way that I would go out dancing in the hopes of meeting a woman whose energy matched my own. I suppose I would have to say that meditation had its own sexual allure: Foreign, beguiling, mysterious and promising release, it beckoned from afar. Casting about for someone or something that I could put my heart into, I was searching, at a critical time of young adulthood, for a connection that would enliven me. The spiritual search and the sexual search were bound up with one another. Perhaps it is for this reason that the split between the two has never seemed quite right to me.

Many of the critical moments that made me feel confident I was on the correct spiritual path felt right because they were charged with an erotic energy that both excited and enticed me, while at the same time making me a bit apprehensive. I remember being at my first *kirtan*, a devotional call-and-response chanting popular in India that Western devotees had brought back to America, and being overwhelmed by the sweet, sad beauty of the music just as I was swayed by the radiant attractiveness of the musicians on the stage. Young Americans just back from India, the musicians were cloaked in shimmering

Asian garb and appeared, to my impressionable gaze, like visitors from some heavenly realm that I had thought existed only in the imagination. Their music captured the poignant longing of the human heart for certainty in the face of the vast ephemerality of the material world while simultaneously giving me the chance to lock eyes with a young beauty across the room whom I later visited at the local Meher Baba ashram and to whom I found I had nothing to say. But this later disappointment did nothing to diminish the impact of that first opening. The music touched something in me that went very deep, a longing that had both erotic and spiritual qualities, that felt very personal and yet completely new and strange. While the Hindu deities to whom the chants were directed—Shiva, Ganesh, Krishna, Hanuman, Sita and Rama—were unknown to me at the time, the force that was unleashed in the communal supplication seemed irresistible.

There was something in my initial flirtation with Eastern spirituality that awakened me to the power of longing. Kama's flowered arrows flew at me in a rush. I felt invited to touch desire, or at least gaze upon it, even while reaching for what might be called loftier spiritual heights. I was perplexed by this at first, since many of my more formal spiritual teachings—drawn from the right-handed approach—promised that meditation was the antidote to passion, not a catalyst of it, but the truth was too powerful to ignore.

Meditation and yoga, like most religious practices around the world, are built on renunciation, and see lusting after sensory gratification as bondage to the wheel of suffering. Many of the vows that Buddhist monks, or *bhikkhus*, were required to take were designed to protect them from temptation, to stop desire from obscuring the clear perception of things. According to certain teachings of Buddhist psychology, one of the routes to true happiness is to learn how to remove the filter of idealization that creates distorted mental images of our objects of affection. These distortions often lead to disappointment, because the actual reality can never live up to the idealized one.

Buddhism has, until its entry into the West, been primarily a monastic discipline and, like all of India's religions, it puts great emphasis on the importance of renunciation and asceticism. The classic Buddhist poem, the *Dhammapada*, has verses about desire that speak of its dangerous nature, verses that a monk (or *bhikkhu*) was expected to know by heart.

> *Craving is like a creeper,*
> *it strangles the fool.*
> *He bounds like a monkey, from one birth to another,*
> *looking for fruit. . . .*

> *Thirty-six streams of sense flow in a man*
> *looking for pleasure.*
> *They seek passion,*
> *their waves will sweep him away. . . .*

> *Crazed with craving,*
> *men flee like hunted hares.*
> *O* bhikkhu, *freedom comes only*
> *from the conquest of craving.*

> *Look at him!—*
> *Having conquered the forest of desire,*
> *he runs to the forest of new desires;*
> *freed from the forest of desire,*

he runs to the forest of new desires.
—All in vain; for he runs into bondage. . . .

Weeds are the poison of fields
and desire the poison of man.
Honor the man without desire
and earn high reward.[5]

But while this is the face that is presented for public consumption, and the one most appropriate for monastic existence, my experience suggested something more complex. For as I practiced meditation with increasing vigor, peeking through the dusty draperies of routinized thought into the raw immediacy of my own physical presence in the world, my desire became more and more apparent, rather than more subdued. While many people engaged in meditation claimed to find that it made them more relaxed, I made a somewhat different discovery. Admittedly anxious to begin with, I stumbled on a rather odd realization: The opposite of anxiety is not calmness, it is desire.

Anxiety and desire are two, often conflicting, orientations to the unknown. Both are tilted toward the future. Desire implies a willingness, or a need, to engage this unknown, while anxiety suggests a fear of it. Desire takes one out of oneself, into the possibility of relationship, but it also takes one deeper into oneself. Anxiety turns one back on oneself, but only onto the self that is already known. There is nothing mysterious about the anxious state; it leaves one teetering in an untenable and all too familiar isolation. There is rarely desire without some associated anxiety: We seem to be wired to have apprehension about that which we cannot control, so in this way, the two are not really complete opposites. But desire gives one a reason to tolerate anxiety and a willingness to push through it.

Meditation did not relieve me of my anxiety so much as flesh it out. It took my anxious response to the world, about which I felt a lot of confusion and shame, and let me understand it more completely. Perhaps the best way to phrase it is to say that meditation showed me that the other side of anxiety is desire. They exist in relationship to each other, not independently.

FEED EVERYONE

While this might have been disturbing, I was not as confused by it as I might have been. I was helped in this, I think, by two fortunate circumstances. The first involved serendipitous relationships that developed with several of the first Westerners to bring Buddhism to this country, who shared some of their own personal struggles and helped me to feel less strange about the chaotic underpinnings of my mind that were uncovered in those early years of practice. These friends and teachers alerted me to an underlying, and sometimes partially hidden, theme in Eastern spirituality in which the sensuous is not set up as the enemy but is linked with the sacred. In my early immersion in Indian thought, I found hints of a culture that did not separate the two from each other. Before I ever traveled there, I was awakened to the transformational potential of this alternative universe through interactions with one of my first spiritual teachers, a Jewish professor of psychology turned Hindu guru named Ram Dass. In a trajectory that, in my own more subdued way, I repeated, Ram Dass (born Richard Alpert) left the department of psychology at Harvard and journeyed to India in search of Eastern teachers of spiritual wisdom. I never had him as a psychology professor—he had been forced out before I arrived at Harvard—but, like footsteps in winter snow, his legacy could still be found. When I first met him, months shy of my twenty-first birthday, one of his favorite stories was about a conversation with his Indian guru that began with a single, and ancient, question, "How can I know God?"

There was a plaintive quality to the story, since at other times, when speaking of his guru, Ram Dass seemed convinced that his teacher *was* God. I can imagine him, though, asking God how he could know God. The ego can never be sure enough, it seems.

In any case, the answer that came back to Ram Dass was an interesting one.

"Feed everyone," his guru, Neem Karoli Baba, replied without hesitation.

As someone whose family took pride in their parsimonious dinner portions and their absence of dessert, I was intrigued by the idea of the importance of food. Didn't the spiritual path demand abstinence? What did eating have to do with wisdom? What kind of yoga was feeding people? Why was Ram Dass always repeating this story? Didn't he know that meditation was the true path to knowledge? Thoughts like these always seemed to accompany my hearing of this story. I assumed the tale was meant in some kind of metaphorical way, until I visited his teacher's temple and saw for myself.

Some years after I first heard Ram Dass recount this vignette, I traveled to India for the dedication of a *murti*, or monument, in Vrindavan to his guru's memory. Vrindavan is known as the birthplace of Krishna, a holy city in the north of India whose very ground is worshipped as the body of the blue-skinned god. Neem Karoli Baba's temple was one of hundreds in the town, but true to his teachings, its dedication was an opportunity for a huge feast. Great vats of food were prepared by his Indian devotees, endless trays of *chapatis* lining the temple's verandah. Longtime followers of Maharaj-ji (the more familiar name for the guru) took the honor of serving lunch to the crowds. People came from all over the city and countryside and waited patiently for their portions, lines snaking outside the temple courtyard as far as the eye could see. An air of quiet celebration, of peaceful satiety, dominated. There was enough for everyone, even the dogs.

In the sheer multitude of the population, the scene reminded me of Satyajit Ray's film *Distant Thunder*, in which large masses of Indian villagers are seen moving majestically over parched red earth fleeing drought and famine. But at Maharaj-ji's temple they were not fleeing, they were coming together. And they were being fed.

It is interesting that Krishna, in whose birthplace Maharaj-ji dwelt, is the god of bingeing without purging. From the time of his childhood, he was known affectionately as the butter thief—"butter" being the term for the curdled milk he was so fond of. People used to hide in the kitchen to watch the small blue-skinned child steal from the butter jar, so great was his pleasure at the taste. His desire was so pure, and his enjoyment so thorough, that watching him eat evoked ecstasy in the onlookers. There was no residue to Krishna's enjoyment, no leftover dissatisfaction or guilt or shame. His desire was not just a reminder of God's blessings, it *was* a blessing in itself.

At times, it seemed as if Krishna would eat anything. His mother once pulled him off the ground in horror when she saw him eating the very dirt of the village. She pried open his mouth to look inside and suddenly found herself staring into a mountain where his uvula should have been, a lake in his right tonsil. The entire universe of which she, herself, was a part, swirled within the baby god's mouth. The Lord was, indeed, one. He gave meaning to the phrase, "We are the world." Krishna had the capacity to meet desire head on and satisfy it completely. In feeding himself, he managed to make everyone feel better.

Maharaj-ji's injunction to Ram Dass, "Feed everyone," made me think about the relationship of desire to the divine. What was he trying to get Ram Dass to see? Certainly, the holiness of the act of giving, of feeding the hungry, of serving God through service to His creatures, is a spiritual message common to all of the world's religions. But I can't help thinking that Maharaj-ji was pointing to something even more specific, something preserved in the age-old story of the baby Krishna. We can know God *in the act* of feeding everyone, and while being fed. Touching desire, meeting and gratifying another's desire, lets us know God. Even such a simple desire as hunger, the foundation of our basic needs, is a window into the vastness of the universe, as Krishna's mother found when she pried open his dirt-smeared little mouth.

The only other event that I witnessed in India to rival the scope of the feast at Maharaj-ji's temple happened when the Dalai Lama came to Bodh Gaya, where the Buddha was enlightened twenty-five hundred years before. Early in the morning, before his first day of teaching, the Dalai Lama gave money away to all who came. Somehow the word must have gotten out, because before dawn I was awakened by clouds of dust rising from the feet of the crowds descending on his tent. This event was no abstract cultivation of generosity or loving kindness, nor was it an offering of teachings on wisdom: It was alms-giving on a mammoth scale. The bodhisattva of compassion, of whom the Dalai Lama was reputed to be an incarnation, was literally giving away rupees, and the response from the local population was overwhelming.

Both of these celebrations had the effect of challenging my preconceptions about the spiritual life. It had been easier for me to understand the path of renunciation than the one of generosity, the right-handed path rather than the left-handed one. One of the things that made the ascetic vision more palatable to me was the tendency, rife in our culture, to view happiness through the prism of Puritanism. In this way of thinking, spiritual happiness is separate from physical happiness, and the only possible approaches to sensual pleasure are indulgence, which is anti-spiritual, or suppression. There is no reverence for the enlightening potential of eros in this view; it is reduced to, at best, one of the lower steps on a ladder that reaches, through renunciation or sublimation, toward the heavens.

Experiences like these kept me open to the possibility that my recovery—or discovery—of desire was not a complete anomaly. As the Dalai Lama has described it, "In the early Buddhist traditions, desire was viewed as a poison to be avoided. The later Mahayana view was not to avoid the poison, but to antidote it with the appropriate remedy. In *Tantra*, desire is seen as a potent energy to be used on the path to enlightenment; just as peacocks in the jungle thrive on poisonous plants and transform them symbolically into the radiant plumage of their tail feathers."[6]

But the more intense teaching was to come several years later, just after entering into the most important love relationship of my adult life, when my soon-to-be wife and I began to turn the wheel of our own *dharma*. The moment crept up on me unawares. I was not looking for any big lesson, I was simply hoping for a little rest and relaxation.

ECSTASY

Several months after my wife and I first fell in love, in a period of time that is now some twenty or more years past, we went for a week's vacation to a beach in Jamaica. While it was not a honeymoon, it was the first extended and uninterrupted time we were to spend with one another since we had met. I had been to Jamaica once before, eight or nine years previously, when the beach in Negril was just being discovered, so I had some picture in my mind's eye of the kind of accommodations that might be possible for us. While I had slept in a shed in someone's backyard on my first visit, I knew that a rather developed tourist industry had taken root in the intervening years. I did not think that it would be difficult to find a setting that would do justice to my desire.

Our trip got off to an unexpectedly difficult start, however. In my zeal to have things perfectly arranged, I had made reservations in the States through a travel agency specializing in Jamaican tourism. I trusted the travel agent and had, in fact, double-checked with a friend who had recently been to Jamaica that the recommended place was a good one.

"You'll be fine there," he had said, and I immediately visualized the view of the beach.

Having put down a hefty deposit, I was horrified when we arrived at what seemed to be nothing more than a windowless cinderblock garage set in a dusty field populated by barking dogs. I could not imagine a bleaker setting. My wife gamely did her best to put a good face on the situation; she led me into the room, looked around and pronounced it fine; but I was aghast. This was not what I had imagined! Although we had been traveling for the better part of the day and the sun was already low in the June sky, I insisted that we pick up our bags and leave that instant. We were without a car, however, having been dropped off by taxi, and we had no choice, if we were to search for a more accommodating environment, but to go trudging down the beach on foot.

Luckily for us, after a bit of a walk, we found a comfortable place called the Charrella Inn, and, with enormous relief, we settled in for our stay. The inn overlooked the shore, and our bedroom, upstairs from the main dining room, looked out at the water and sky from several large curtained windows. Although it was June, and therefore very warm, everything was just fine. Over the next few days, we ate pineapple, explored the local restaurants, lolled on the beach and embraced in the turquoise waters, letting the rest of the world fade deep into the background as we reveled in each other's presence. I was happier than I had ever been.

There was only one thing nagging at me. Back in Cambridge, some six months before, a friend had given me two capsules of a new substance that people were saying was like a love drug. "It opens your heart," I had heard from more than one source. I had been at a party where most everyone had taken it and, while they were all just sitting around looking much the same as they always did, in the aftermath of their experiences they were all raving about how open it had made them feel. I was intrigued by what I had heard and grateful to my friend for giving me a sample to try with my girlfriend, but I had wanted to wait for the perfect moment. I had been carrying it around in my wallet ever since, wondering when such a moment might present itself.

Now that we were in Jamaica staying in such a nice place, the capsules were burning a hole in my pocket. This was clearly the opportunity I had been waiting for. For several days, as we cavorted in the tropical waters, took our dinners at the local Bar-B-Barn and adjusted to the rhythms of the island, the possibility of feeling *even closer* to my lover tempted me. My wife was indulgent of my wish to explore the drug's effects and trusting of my faith in it. Her attitude toward it was similar to her attitude when we had arrived at the dusty, barren lodgings in Negril. She was willing to give it a try. After about three days we decided to see what would happen.

I remember how excited I was to turn myself over to the drug's effects. It was early morning and the sun was pouring in through the windows. The room was white and the air smelled of the sea. We lay down on the huge bed and waited for something to transpire. We kissed for a while and I felt grateful to be so in love. In the distance I heard the sounds of the breakfast dishes being cleared from below. I soon became very conscious of how hard my heart was beating. The sun was higher in the sky and my body was suddenly pouring with perspiration. My stomach was tight and I felt vaguely nauseated, a metallic taste in my mouth. My wife, while not as symptomatic, was also overtaken by physical pulsations. Everything was throbbing. She pushed me away from her. Neither of us could maintain the physical contact that we had initiated. My skin felt like sandpaper. The tiniest touch was grating and reverberated deep into my nausea. My wish for closeness persisted but was drowned out by the sheer impossibility of the slightest brush against my skin. I was like a Geiger counter, picking up the tiniest bits of radiation. It was a hot day, and I heard the unmistakable whine of mosquitoes. I have a tremendous aversion to mosquitoes, but I could do nothing to protect myself from them. The air in the room felt very close. We were immobilized on the bed, unable to touch, all of our effort going into the simple act of breathing. Several times I crawled to the bathroom to vomit. It did not get better.

My wife was able to maintain her sense of humor, but I was filled with remorse. "Don't ever listen to me again," I implored her, ready to forsake any remnant of spiritual authority that my excursions to India might have afforded me. "I don't know anything," I insisted repetitively, as the sun arced through the Jamaican sky. I felt like a fool. As sunset approached, we wobbled down the stairs to get some tea or soup. The day had evaporated. I had wasted our precious time together.

The day's circumstances left me questioning myself in a profound way. Already so in love, I had wanted it to be *more*. But my reaching for more had given me less. I was, as the saying goes, hoist by my own petard. In trying to forge a perfect union, I had undercut a union that was already perfect enough. While I did not find what I was expecting, I had a major revelation that day in Jamaica. I learned that if I was going to pursue the path of desire, I had better not be in such a rush. I would have to get to know the space between us just as intimately as everything else.

LORD OF OBSTACLES

This event has rolled back and forth over me for the past twenty-odd years. It crystallized something about love and desire that I am still struggling to accept. Up until that point, I had assumed that love was driving toward union. There could be nothing higher than the merger of lover and beloved. I never questioned the truth of this assumption, and was always oriented, one way or another, toward accessing, whenever or however possible, this imagined state of interconnection or unity. At various times in my life, I had experiences that affirmed this basic notion. Now that I was engaged in a full-fledged love affair, a more sustainable merging seemed possible, one that could be driven both by sexual desire *and* by love.

But the fallacies of my assumptions were suddenly as vivid, and unavoidable, as the whine of the mosquitoes had been. In the repetitions of "I don't know anything" that flowed out of me in the aftermath of our experience, I was admitting to something very difficult. There was a flaw in my understanding of union. Somehow, in my desire to merge with my beloved, I was looking to get rid of my self. I was not content to take things as they came in our relationship, I wanted to throw myself so completely into it that I would be completely out of it. The drug, for whatever reason, refused to accommodate me. It threw me back into myself with such force that I was reeling from the pain of it. It made me suddenly very appreciative of the much more tenuous and endlessly shifting union that sometimes emerged between us. This was a place, a state or an energy field, where nobody disappeared but where both of us were quite transformed, a place of "co-creation and mutual recognition," as an analyst named Jessica Benjamin has described it.[7] What more did I want?

My interest in recreational drugs faded after that day, and, while it is far from true that my desire for merger entirely disappeared, my unquestioning belief in oneness as some kind of absolute attainable perfection was dealt a severe blow. Instead, I began to imagine an alternative scenario, one in which separation and union are not inevitable opposites but two intrinsic aspects of one love, part of the constant ebb and flow, like the Jamaican waters surrounding us, that describe intimacy. What I have come to understand is that in the intensity of my love, I was able to experience something of the truth of the Buddha's teachings about the ultimate emptiness of the self. As pundits throughout the ages have affirmed, it is easy when in love to loosen the bonds of the self. As I have already remarked, even in Tibetan Buddhism, the analogy that is always used to describe the truth of "no-self" is that of orgasm. The self falls away effortlessly under the spell of love. But I was not yet able to take this realization back home. In relying on "union" with my lover to give me the taste of this experience, I was clinging unnecessarily to a single manifestation of this truth. I needed to find it within myself, as well as with her. Ecstasy might also be something that could come from the inside.

In the world of Indian mythology, there is a god for this kind of lesson. There is a god for almost everything, in fact; that is one of the revelations of India, the way the sacred is infused so completely with the everyday world. The god I am thinking of is one of the most beloved of all, the elephant-headed Ganesh. Ganesh is popularly known as the remover of obstacles. He is propitiated at the beginnings of things: when initiating a new project, a period of worship, a pilgrimage, or a journey; even at weddings, the beginning of married life. He would have been watching when the Buddha set the wheel of *dharma* rolling, and he would have been chuckling as my wife and I struggled to get our relationship on the right track. He is a doorkeeper who guards the thresholds of space and time.[8]

But even in this capacity, things are not what we think. There are what we might call "higher" teachings. Like desire, Ganesh is not simple. He is not really the "remover" of obstacles, it turns out; he is more properly referred to as the "Lord" of obstacles. He does not just clear impediments away, he creates them. As an adherent of desire, Ganesh is a guardian of the threshold between old and new, but he also occupies the border between lover and beloved. He sits in the liminal space, in the gap between. His form is not quite animal and not exactly human, not quite human and not exactly divine.[9] He is like us when we are in love. Not so sure what he is, but happy to be there.

Like desire itself, Ganesh is a mass of contradictions. He is a stocky, corpulent presence, but he is often shown dancing, balancing on a single limb. He is huge, but he rides upon a mouse. He carries a radish in one hand and a plate of sweetmeats in another, but also a goad, a hatchet and a noose. Elephant-headed though he may be, he is also the most literate of the gods, transcribing the entire epic of the *Mahabharata*, one of the oldest and most beautiful lyric poems in the world, the Indian equivalent of the *Iliad*.

Ganesh is held in particular reverence, even today. Occasionally, there are news reports from remote areas of India that a statue is drinking the milk that has been left as an offering for him. In such august institutions as Sotheby's or Christie's, major auction houses in New York City for classical Asian art, the statues of Ganesh are invariably adorned with anonymous offerings of money and flowers, surreptitiously placed there by passing patrons. On a recent visit to Christie's, in fact, a guard alerted me to the potency of one particular twelfth-century Ganesh, on whose lap a vast fortune seemed to be accumulating. "Make sure you ask for something," the guard whispered under his breath. The array spread out before the statue reminded me of the peppers surrounding the weeping Nasruddin in his Middle Eastern marketplace. Money, chocolates and flower petals, rather than peppers, spilled out before him. Desire seems to prompt such displays. In Nasruddin's case the taste of the display was hot and spicy, and in this situation the flavor was undoubtedly sweet, but the thought of both together made me aware, once again, of the power that desire has to create such contradictory feelings in us.

Desire teaches us, not just by gratification, but by constantly undercutting itself, by never being entirely satisfied. It rubs our faces in reality by always falling a bit short of its goal. This is desire's secret agenda, to alert us to the gap between our expectations and the way things actually are. In so doing, it shows us that there is something more interesting than success or failure, more compelling than having complete control. As I discovered on the beach in Jamaica, I thought I was directing things, but I was not in charge. I had a lesson to learn that I was not anticipating. I could almost see Ganesh, the Lord of Obstacles, balancing precariously on a mouse, swaying from side to side, rolling his eyes at me.

"Love is trickier than you think," he wanted me to understand, before my marriage had even begun. To free desire from the tendency to cling, we have to be willing to stumble over ourselves.

Our tendency, under the spell of longing, is to try to take possession of that which we crave, to try to *fix* it, in both senses of the word. We want to preserve that which we desire, freeze it or trap it, the way photographic chemicals fix an image that has been developed. And we want to improve it, take the problem of elusiveness away, make desire less likely to cause us dismay. We want to fix the runaway quality that has us always in a chase.

But desire does not relinquish its mystery so easily. It has something else in store for us. Where possession is not possible, love can grow. Ganesh, the doorkeeper, guards the entrance to the human heart.

3

Discontent

As Ganesh makes clear, for something so apparently straightforward, desire is remarkably complicated. In its relentless pursuit of passion and pleasure, in its striving forever onward, desire keeps thrusting us into unknown territory, undercutting our needs for stability, security and certainty. At the same time, desire craves exactly those qualities of stability, security and certainty that it simultaneously undermines. Like a Zen master's *koan*—a question whose answer cannot be found with the rational mind—desire forces us into a place where our usual modes of relating are upended, where success can only be found when, like Nasruddin, we risk making fools of ourselves. This seems to be one of desire's primary functions: to keep us off balance, in between, on the verge, or just out of reach. For all of our attachments to pleasure, this is an uncomfortable place to dwell. But as many a Zen master has come to appreciate, there is value in being uncomfortable. If we learn to attend to it in a meditative manner, it can bring us to the state of openness and stillness that Buddhism so values. The kind of discomfort that desire engenders is actually closer to what the Buddhists see as reality than the more assured position that we mask ourselves with. Balance comes when we learn to be off balance, not when we hold ourselves aloof. It is from this place that our inner life grows.

If the essence of Zen is paradox, then the essence of desire is certainly Zen. In Zen, as in all the other schools of Buddhism, there is a special interest in that which is ordinarily ignored, especially if it makes us a little uncomfortable. "In Zen they say, 'If something is boring for two minutes, try it for four. If still boring, try it for eight, sixteen, thirty-two, and so on,'" said the Zen-inspired composer John Cage. That which is overlooked or underappreciated is food for Zen thought. It might be the sound of the breeze, the reflection of the sky in the early morning dew or the washing of a breakfast bowl. It might be a cup of tea or the picking of weeds in the garden, helping a child with homework or folding the laundry. Attention to these simple, omnipresent facts of our existence is the (methodless) method of Buddhist meditation, the beginning of an integration of meditative insight with daily life. Rather than rushing past these seemingly useless experiences in search of something more meaningful, Zen counsels us to pay attention to the everyday.

When it ventures into the world of human relationships, as it does in the left-handed path, Buddhism continues to emphasize attention to the whole picture, not just the parts that we idealize. This is the core principle of the path of desire, the one that turns affairs of the heart into spiritual fodder. John Cage made music from silence as well as from musical instruments. He brought attention, in just this way, to the overlooked spaces between the notes. Trained in the discipline of not recoiling from that which is unpleasant, and not cleaving to that which is pleasant, the Buddhist approach is to investigate whatever is given. In the case of desire, what is given includes the gap between satisfaction and fulfillment, the loneliness that persists even in love. Intrigued by this gap in both my personal life and in my work as a psychotherapist, I have found it to be as rich a source of inspiration as the imagined union of lover and beloved. Delving into it permits an appreciation of desire that is possible only when its paradoxical nature is acknowledged. While it may not take us to where we think it should, desire can, in the Buddhist approach, take us all the way to nirvana.

A patient of mine, a photographer in his mid-thirties named Mike whose meditation practice was beginning to mature, came to my office recently and told me the following story. Coming downtown to see me on the subway, he noticed a young woman standing in the car across the aisle from where he was sitting. She had a beautiful body that he could not help but admire, held tightly in a pair of white jeans. He sat across the crowded car gazing up and down at her, commenting to himself about how it was too bad her face was not as beautiful as her body. Suddenly another woman called out to her—she seemed to know her from when she was younger—"Tanya, how have you been? How's your family? Are you still singing as much as you were?" Mike was taken up short. He saw that the young woman was no more than about seventeen years old and he felt bad about the way he was objectifying her.

"I suddenly realized there was a whole person there," he

confided. "When I was looking at her before, it was like I was erasing her personhood."

Mike and the woman got off at the same stop and Mike noticed, as he walked out of the car, that he reflexively turned—even after his realization—to try to get one last look at her body.

"I couldn't believe it," Mike said. "The whole thing reminded me of how I caught myself last night after having Chinese food eating a fortune cookie. I just smashed the whole thing in my mouth—pieces all over the floor—like an animal, and I caught myself, 'What am I doing?' And I knew, 'This is how I'm living my life; just skimming the surface of things. There's not enough depth to the way I am living.'"

Mike's story made me smile. I liked that he could admit how lustily he looked at the young woman, and how helpless he was not to take that last glance. But I also appreciated his humility upon recognizing her humanity, and his willingness to speak of the conflict it created in him. His ability to make use of the serendipitous event on the subway to examine the way he was letting desire push him around was impressive. Without pushing his desire away, he was beginning to let it transform.

THE GAP

Some people imagine that there is no desire in Buddhism, or that the point is to eliminate desire altogether. But Mike's story provides a truer picture. His meditative practice allowed his desire to become an object of contemplation. He was starting to emerge, through the power of his own self-observation, from a state of being run by desire to one that could be less hurried, less frantic and less demeaning to himself and others. My daughter has a textbook of world history with a chapter on

Buddhism in it that presents a view of Buddhism incompatible with the subtleties of Mike's opening. Her school teaches from this text in the ninth grade—the chapter on Buddhism comes right at the beginning of the book. It looks so simple when it is written in print. "The Buddha taught that the cause of suffering is desire and that the way to end suffering is to end desire." Stop desire, stop suffering. What could be clearer? I tried to tell my daughter that it was more complicated than that, however.

"The Buddha taught that the cause of suffering is *craving,*" I told her, "not desire. There is a difference between them. Or you could say the cause is *clinging,*" I added helpfully, helplessly watching as her teenaged eyes glazed over with disdain. She was not interested in the subtleties. What they said in the book was good enough for her. That was all she needed to know for the upcoming test. On to Jainism, nonviolence, *ahimsa.* Like desire, itself, she was ready for the next thing.

Even in Buddhism, of course, there is a goal that is desired, one that is common to both right-handed and left-handed paths. This goal has to do with being fully present in the moment, aware without judgment and able to live fully in the Now. But as many a meditator has belatedly had to admit, even this goal is impossible to achieve. The present moment is always dissolving. Neurologically speaking, there is a lag of at least a third of a second between the "present" moment and our ability to be conscious of it. Even the present is constantly running away from us. One contemporary American Zen master describes it the following way. "To be present in the midst of being what we are is a pure sensation that we can never exactly apprehend. It is fleeting and ungraspable."[1] *A pure sensation that we can never exactly apprehend.* Ever elusive, the object of desire, even in Zen, is continually receding.

This realization has led to a refreshing kind of humility in the Buddhist imagination with regard to desire, an ease and acceptance of its discordant nature that does not seem natural to our Western minds. There is a story about the Dalai Lama on one of his first visits to Los Angeles. He was teaching there for a week, and each day was driven back and forth past the same row of fancy shops, showcasing the latest in technological gadgets. By the end of the week, he said, he wanted these things, even though he didn't know what they were![2] What hope is there of eliminating desire altogether if even the Dalai Lama has such a response?

While there are certainly strains within Buddhism that have interpreted things exactly as my daughter's textbook described them, this is not the most felicitous understanding to have emerged from twenty-five hundred years of wrestling with the problem. Once it became clear that not only could desire never be entirely eliminated but also that it could never be entirely satiated, a different relationship to it had to be worked out. Like an insistent and irrepressible child, desire pushes us until we accept it for what it is. And it is a wonderful teacher. The more successful it is at realizing its goal, the more it opens us up to its failure.

There is a famous story from Japan that expresses the peculiar delight with which desire is held in the Buddhist tradition.[3] A young woman, it is told, is walking through a field when she encounters a tiger that eyes her hungrily. She runs and the tiger pursues her. She comes to a cliff, takes hold of the root of a wild vine and, in a single motion, swings herself over the precipice. Dangling there, clutching the vine, she sees the tiger sniffing the ground above her. Trembling, she looks down. It is a long way to the bottom, and she feels momentarily dizzy. Then she sees something else. There is another tiger below, presumably a hungry one, who has also noticed her plight. The tigers prowl, one above and one below, waiting for their feast. She clings to the vine. Suddenly, two mice appear at the edge of the cliff and start to gnaw at the roots that hold her. The woman notices a wild strawberry growing nearby on the side of the hill. She reaches with one hand to pluck the strawberry, still clutching the vine with the other, and places the fruit in her mouth. She takes one bite. Ahhhh! How sweet it tastes.

This is the end of the story. We never learn what happens—or, rather, we are told exactly what we need to hear. The story, as I understand it, is about desire. As a Buddhist teaching story, it is obviously about other things as well. It is about being in the moment and the fragility of everyday life and doing one thing at a time, but it also seems to be a metaphor for desire. The woman encounters her desire and it appears as a tiger. In psychoanalysis, the tiger would be called a projection. Fierce, wild, devouring. A beast. Just as with desire, there seem to be only two options: to flee or to surrender to it.

Our protagonist runs from the beast, only to encounter a second tiger. There is no escape. Cornered, she hangs on for dear life. But desire continues to torment her. It changes form, multiplies, threatens her as she struggles to avoid it. Even in the form of the mice it is dangerous. How can she escape? The solution lies in the strawberry. What does she do? She tastes it and it is good. She takes one bite, not even knowing if she will have a second one, not knowing if there will be a next moment at all. With complete attention, she savors the flavor of the fruit. Desire is the tiger and the mouse, but it is also the strawberry. When the young woman stops running and gives up the fear of being devoured, she can finally taste it. The flavor of desire is good.

There are fruits to dropping into the gap, the story suggests. Trying to weed out discomfort from our experience of desire only makes it more overwhelming. But allowing oneself to fall into the space that desire cannot span makes the experience complete. The little bit of lack that remains, after even the most satisfying resolution of desire, is a window into something important, something true. While we are conditioned to recoil from this elusiveness, to see it as a deficiency that must be overcome, it is possible to relate to it in a completely different way. It can actually be enjoyed as an inextricable, and ineluctable, aspect of desire's nature, and a window into the true nature of the self.

Most of the time, however, we are not in good enough emotional shape to taste the flavor of the strawberry. Too often, we are in pursuit of the next thing, trying to escape from the discomfort and disappointment of the last one. Like Ravana in the *Ramayana*, we are endlessly frustrated in our attempts to take complete possession of a desired object. We never learn how to make use of the space between, as Rama and Sita are forced to do, as I needed to do after my debacle on the beach in Jamaica, and as my patient Mike began to do while observing himself on the subway.

Our experience of desire is often more complicated and conflicted than the Zen story suggests it has to be. We do not fall willingly into the gap but react to it as if it were an insult. Inevitably left hungry and in pursuit of something more, we begin to cast about for something or someone to blame. Sometimes we blame ourselves, sometimes our loved ones and sometimes desire itself. But as the best Buddhist teachings insist, we do this because we superimpose an extra quality of "objective reality" on that which we desire. When Mike was eyeing the young woman on the subway, in his fantasies he was making her "his." There was no room, until her old friend called out, for him to appreciate her subjective reality. In a similar manner, when I was struggling to become one with my wife in Jamaica, I was assuming that she had some "essence" that I needed to possess. Her unreachability felt like a problem, not something to celebrate.

Grasping onto the extrinsic appearance of things, we expect to be satisfied in a complete way. We look to union or merger, as I did with my wife, as the antidote to our suffering. But this kind of satisfaction is impossible because the qualities that we project onto the desired object—of permanence, stability or "thingness"—do not really exist. As a result, we are inevitably disappointed. The disparity between the way we perceive things and the way they actually are is at the root of our struggle with desire. Once we learn how to make that disparity part of our experience, however, desire can be a teacher rather than an affliction. We can open to it more when we stop fighting with the way it disappoints us.

BITTERSWEET

This is an insight that can be traced back, not just to the ancient Indian civilizations, but also to the ancient Greeks. The poet and scholar Anne Carson, in a brilliant essay on eros, summons the Greek lyrical poets to get a sense of the paradox that desire inevitably comes up against. She quotes a fragment of one of Sappho's verses in which desire is described, not as sweet like the strawberry, but as "bittersweet." Bittersweet is our English word, but as Carson retranslates the poem, she shows us that Sappho actually called it "sweetbitter"—the sweetness comes first, then the bite.

> *Eros once again limb-loosener whirls me*
> *sweetbitter, impossible to fight off, creature stealing up*[4]

The quality of taste is not actually the initial thing to strike us in this remarkable passage. Sappho first captures desire's relentless quality. *Eros once again*, she intones, helplessness not far from the surface. Then she moves to the otherworldly, almost impersonal, quality of desire and the way it takes us over. *Creature stealing up*, impossible to fight off, whirling us, it loosens our limbs and makes us do things we never thought we were capable of. Almost as an afterthought, the "sweetbitter" flavor floats to the surface. It is a complicated experience.

As Carson interprets it, there is a "mingling" quality to desire; it makes us feel how both poles of affect can be united in a single experience, how opposites are not opposites but two sides of the same coin. "Love and hate converge within erotic desire,"[5] she notes, echoing the insights of many of today's most experienced couples therapists. Why should this be? Carson is explicit about the reason. "Desire can only be for what is lacking," she explains. Because it is predicated on lack, stimulated by separation and always coming up against reality, it is destined to fall short, or at least to be dissatisfied with whatever it finds.

Freud was as moved by this truth as Sappho. As the founder of psychoanalysis, he sat in his consulting room and watched his patients' desires unfold before his eyes. More than most people, he refrained from judgment about what he saw. The therapist, he declared, should "give impartial attention to everything there is to observe."[6] Although he did not know it, these are the same instructions that the Buddha gave to his monks as he taught them to listen to themselves. Peeking beneath the surface of Victorian repression, Freud discovered a torrent of libido, which he described with as much incredulity as his Greek forebears, coming to essentially the same conclusions.

"It is the difference in amount between the pleasure of satisfaction which is *demanded* and that which is actually *achieved* that provides the driving factor which will permit no halting at any position attained,"[7] he concluded. We are driven forward, Freud felt, by a deceitful master, ever promising ultimate satisfaction and ever incapable of coming through. What are we looking for from sex, Freud wanted to know; what are we *demanding* of it? What is it about pleasure that is not satisfying? We seem to be seeking a level of relief that is not available, and we get angry when it does not come. Freud's puzzlement was evident as he confronted this reality.

"There is so often associated with the erotic relationship, over and above its own sadistic components, a quota of plain inclination to aggression. The love-object will not always view these complications with the degree of understanding and tolerance shown by the peasant woman who complained that her husband did not love her any more, since he had not beaten her for a week."[8]

In Freud's humor we find him probing the same phenomenon as Sappho and Anne Carson. As much as desire promises deliverance, it also disappoints. Yet this disappointment is necessary for desire to be maintained. What kind of a system is this? It is a catch-22. A double-bind. Desire's survival is dependent on its frustration. Just when it appears to have reached its goal, it seeks out something else to covet. It never knows when to stop. And we are the vehicles of this endless drama. *Impossible to fight off*, desire whirls us *once again*. As if churning butter, desire molds us in its own image. *Sweetbitter*.

As the renouncers of the world's religions have concluded, it is a frightening prospect to be completely under desire's spell. But as the practitioners of the yoga of desire have discovered, the disappointment inherent in desire can be interesting. It deepens our inner lives, makes us grow and illuminates the true nature of reality.

Despite our best intentions, desire continually wafts us into a peculiar kind of gap. As Anne Carson portrays it, there are three characters in any story of eros, "lover, beloved and that which comes between them."[9] This third character, the obstacle that comes between, is the critical factor in the path of desire. This is where one of the most helpful Buddhist teachings begins to make sense. The obstacle that comes between is always clinging. And clinging is driven by the hope that something or someone, somewhere, has some kind of ultimate reality.

When desire is made into an object of contemplation, it always reveals an uncomfortable, but ultimately liberating, truth. Neither lover, nor beloved, has the solidity that we assume is required. The gap that comes between lover and beloved is a reflection of this lack of solidity. We want to possess, or be possessed; but nothing is substantial enough, lasting enough, permanent enough or *real enough*, to ultimately come through. In Buddhist language, it is said that nothing is real enough *in its own right* to be ultimately satisfying. Indeed, the transcendence that desire seeks can only be found by accepting this.

However much we might protest, there is always something that comes between. There was no way for Sita to avoid Ravana's objectification of her. My own clinging managed to keep me apart from my wife in Jamaica. Mike's devouring of the fortune cookie kept him from savoring it. While the circumstances are always kaleidoscopically changing, the result is nonetheless the same. Desire must confront the gap that our clinging wishes to eradicate. How we handle this gap makes all the difference in our own unfolding lives. Sappho's verse, like Freud's musings, washes us up on its shores. Do we weep but persevere like Nasruddin? Take the bitter with the sweet like Sappho? Or can we approach it in yet another way? Both Sappho and Nasruddin hint at the Buddha nature of desire.

WRITTEN IN STONE

Once this alternative view of desire is conceived, it is easy to see evidence of it everywhere. In the first major monuments built in the centuries after the Buddha's death, an effort was made to express the essence of his wisdom in sculptural form. It was an attempt to write in stone what the Buddha had asked his followers to know in their hearts. For a movement built on an appreciation of transience and ephemerality, these structures were something of a contradiction. But their massiveness did not stop them from manifesting the essential truth about the nature of desire: its inability ever to reach its object completely. These monuments, called *stupas*, were solid, monolithic circular stone edifices, built in the style of even more ancient Indian burial mounds. They were constructed, at least originally, to contain relics of the Buddha's body or his ashes, and they came to represent his death, his final entry into nirvana and the clarity of his enlightened mind. The paradox of their form, however, was that there was no way to reach their center. One could only circle them, in a kind of ritual circumambulation that came to be a form of meditation in itself.

A great railing surrounded the stupa, as large, in some cases, as several hundred feet in diameter, in a style that dates from ancient railings that once surrounded sacred trees or shrines. The railing, which was carved on both its inner and outer faces, created a sacred area between the periphery and the inner mound. Four elaborately carved gateways, each at ninety degrees remove, allowed entrance to this enclosed area, where people would come to circle the stupa in a clockwise direction, doing a form of walking meditation prescribed by the Buddha.

It is said that Ashoka, the third century B.C. Buddhist emperor of India, built 84,000 stupas after his conversion from a warrior king to a peace-loving Buddhist ruler. But Ashoka's stupas were just the beginning. All over India, at sites that had fallen into obscurity before being rediscovered by archaeologists in the eighteenth and nineteenth centuries, are scattered monuments from the turn of the millennium two thousand years ago that express, architecturally, the Buddha's teachings. The largest and most important are at places called Sanchi (third–first century B.C.), Bharhut (c. 100 B.C.) and Amaravati (first–second century A.D.), but they arose everywhere the gradually evolving new religion took hold.

One of the consistent motifs in all of the stupas is the presence, on the outside of the railing and the exterior of the four major gates, of sensuous male and female forms, often intertwined with vines, trees, flowers, other vegetation and each other. The lushness of the imagery is amazing. The gates and railings are literally teeming with figures, snakes, elephants and what are usually referred to as fertility icons: semi-clad *yakshis* and *yakshas*, female and male personifications of nature spirits; images of prosperity, abundance and sensual satisfaction. Some sculptures show branches emerging from women's vaginas or vines flowing from their navels, others show full-bodied goddesses gently tapping the sides of trees with their toes to bring them to fruition. Couples fondling each other or engaged in sexual intercourse are set off against rondels of lotuses, their soft shimmering petals catching the light, filling the outer pillar walls. The entire effect is one of desire on full display, all of it ushering the visitor into the processional path where meditative circumambulation is performed, circling the ashes of the Buddha.

The presence of these sensual sculptures has long puzzled scholars. What are they doing ringing a Buddhist holy place? The conventional view seems to be that these images are symbols of the transitory world of passions and desires that the individual must leave behind upon entering the temple or *stupa* complex.[10] It is as if the railings demarcate a sacred space, isolating it from the profane world of desire and sensuality that continues outside the temple bounds. But other experts dispute this. While they tend to agree that the sensual figures clearly mark a boundary between profane and sacred, they affirm that the fertility figures were meant to welcome the worshippers. Visitors were required to walk *under* them, they note, to accept their blessings before entering the domain of the Buddha. These fertility figures would have been familiar to the local populace, they were in the culture before the Buddha arrived, and they seem to have been recruited by the temple artists to help visitors feel more at home.[11]

To me, the imagery of desire at these ancient sites makes

sense only if we see it as integrated into the rest of the monument. The enjoyment of sensual desire then becomes the entry point to the Buddha's teachings. It is as close as we can come, in our day-to-day lives, to the blissful consciousness that the Buddha discovered. But sensual desire leaves a gap. This gap is the processional path inside the sumptuously decorated railing, the intermediate space between desire and its object, where meditation takes place. It is a familiar place, this gap; it is the same space that comes between lover and beloved, preventing the merger or union that is yearned for. It is the very gap that the Buddha described when he started the wheel of dharma rolling, the gap between desire and satisfaction that keeps us longing for more.

The architecture of the stupa is designed to highlight this gap, to make it into a place of practice, instead of letting it become a source of frustration. The stupa acknowledges the very compelling joys of sensual desire, but does not let us stop there. We are meant to come closer, into a liminal space where we can feel the incompleteness of desire's demands. Only by acknowledging this incompleteness can we understand the Buddha's ultimate truth: Neither self nor other has the intrinsic identity, the solidity, that we wish for. This realization was the source of the Buddha's enlightenment, and afforded him a profound satisfaction. Like the Buddha's teachings, the stupa creates a space where desire can be held in all of its complexity and ambiguity. And it points to an even greater joy, an even more venerable object of affection: the Buddha's own illumination, shining on his followers the way the sun sparkles down from the sky.

The architecture of the stupa describes a twofold truth about desire. By placing it so close to the center of the monument, the design highlights desire's enlightening potential, the joy that it can bring and the similarity of this joy to that of the Buddha's nirvana. But by making eros the threshold of nirvana, the architecture of the *stupa* also reveals an essential aspect that must be confronted before nirvana can be attained. This is the object's ultimate failure to deliver what is being asked of it. Desire can take you to nirvana, the stupa architecture suggests, but only if you are willing to follow where it leads.

Awareness of desire reveals some uncomfortable truths. Sappho called them sweetbitter, but the Buddha agreed only in a relative way. Yes, desire always disappoints. But if we can make this disappointment the object of our awareness, then desire can become enlightening. As the young woman hanging over the cliff in the Zen story of the strawberry discovered, the gap can be sweet, even if we are at the end of our rope.

· II ·

CLINGING

Lord of Lanka, I am the son of the wind, fast or

slow, irresistible in my cover. I'm an animal;

what you call beauty won't turn my head.

I crossed the ocean, as a person without

attachment to worldly desires easily crosses the

ocean of existence. Withdraw your heart from

Sita, or that will be a costly theft, for it's by her

energy that I jumped over the sea.

Ramayana (p. 259)

4

The Flavor of Separation

One might think that my confrontation with "the obstacle that comes between" on the beach in Jamaica might have been enough for one lifetime. Certainly it showed me the basic fallacy in my understanding of union and the need to spend less time pushing away the gap between self and other. Yet part of my motivation in writing this book is to show how challenging it can be to bring awareness into our daily desire-driven lives. While Ganesh, Lord of Obstacles, seemed to be particularly present in that early encounter, he has not exactly disappeared from my life since then. The tendency to look outside of myself at critical moments has continued to bedevil me. The yoga of desire does not protect from such tendencies. Rather, it encourages us to make them into the path itself.

Sometime over the past summer, I took myself out to lunch

for a lobster roll—a New York City lobster roll, not a Maine one. It was a special treat and it made a big impression on me, especially at first sight. The lobster roll looked glorious. Hefty amounts of delicately seasoned meat on a warm, butter-kissed hot dog roll. A side of crispy french fries. Lucinda Williams playing on the sound system as I, sipping tea at the stainless steel bar, read my newspaper alone, sun dappling the West Village brownstones that crowded the nearly empty eatery.

For some, this might not have been an occasion for much self-scrutiny, let alone a reflection on Indian mythology, but for me it was an event with all kinds of overtones. What was I doing here? This was not my usual lunch.

A thought had brought me to this spot. My children were away at camp. My wife was in her studio. It felt like the first time in more than fifteen years that I was free of any kind of family responsibility. Having worked all morning, I did not have another appointment until 3:15 and I had missed my midday yoga class, finishing too late to make it there on time. Suddenly, I had time on my hands. Not much time, for sure, but more than I had known for longer than I could remember.

I scanned the possibilities in my mind. I could go upstairs and make myself something for lunch. Too boring. I could go around the corner to one of my usual haunts. I was sick of them. Suddenly, it came. "Lobster roll." The succulent ocean flavor simmered insistently in my psyche. Waves beat against me. I felt guilty and enticed. It seemed so self-indulgent. My wife might be jealous, she was working harder than I was right now. What right did I have to seek such pleasure? But once the thought pierced my consciousness, it became irresistible. A friend had planted the seed the day before, telling me about his favorite place to eat these days. There had already been articles in *The New York Times* about the search for the perfect lobster roll. The perfect doughnut, the perfect cupcake, iced green tea with tapioca pearls. The perfect lobster roll, glistening in my mind's eye, suddenly seemed indispensable. Like the golden deer Sita could not resist following, it hovered right outside the protective circle of my usual routine. It was just the thing, I decided. And I even knew where to find it.

Need I complete the story? How often does reality live up to such expectations? The lobster roll was good but not great. I ate it slowly, careful to savor each bite, trying to extract the essence, but it still disappeared before I was satisfied. I wanted the taste to explode in my mouth instead of just languish, but each bite merely confirmed how ordinary it was. The fries were too thin, too crispy, all crunch with no taste. Maybe the lobster wasn't as fresh as it could be, I thought. Maybe a better lobster roll was still possible. Maybe that other place would have a juicier one, with better french fries. My meal ended and I felt a little restless. Once again, my desire had brought me up short.

It should not have surprised me that the lobster roll was a disappointment. There is something in the nature of desire that invites such experiences. I was reminded of a patient I had seen just that morning, a young woman whose boyfriend had come from out of town for a weekend visit. She wasn't crazy about this boyfriend, he wasn't a real long-term prospect for her, but she still enjoyed being with him, at least for the time being.

"I didn't want it to stop," she told me, "but it's not like I wanted it to go on, either."

It was the same with the lobster roll. In a way, I liked it better before I tasted it. Desire does this kind of thing to us: takes us to places that throw us back on ourselves, places where we feel the gap between our imagined enjoyment and the fulfillment actually available, places where we feel betrayed by a lack of possibility. Even as desire moves toward satisfaction, it also seems to move toward dissatisfaction. Paradox is in its nature.

Perhaps it was just a lousy lobster roll, you might argue. And my patient's boyfriend simply wasn't the right person for her. Surely desire doesn't always lead to disappointment. There is such a thing as a satisfying meal, a good conversation, a great vacation, a wonderful movie, or a pleasing encounter with a lover. And what about true love? Yet, if we look carefully, even these experiences can contain the seeds of discontent. Do they give us everything we are looking for? When we finish with them don't we usually want more? Aren't they often more limited than we might like? They fail us in our demands for *total* surrender, *complete* immersion or *indisputable* closeness. We seem to be seeking something out of this world in our pleasures. We want to be "blown away" and find ourselves irritated in the aftermath to be still in the picture. We long to be transported, annihilated, excited or merely aroused, but when it is over we cannot avoid feeling spurned. Desire moves us toward climax, but its resolution is anticlimactic. It can be maintained only if it remains unfulfilled.

THE LONELINESS OF LOVE

Reflecting on my predicament in the aftermath of the lobster roll, I knew that I was up against the reality of the Buddha's First Noble Truth. In the space that had opened in my schedule, I had been suddenly conscious of my aloneness. Rushing to fill the space, I jumped at the first delectable object to cross my mind. Like Ravana spying the lovely Sita, I clung to my object of desire. Deepening my dissatisfaction rather than diminishing it, this craving seemed to backfire.

I suddenly remembered another recent encounter with a patient of mine, a newly married, former dancer named Kyra. Kyra was angry with her husband for ignoring her. He was not being mean or anything, but sometimes he seemed very far away. They did not seem to be having sexual problems, and the time that they spent together still made her happy; there was just not enough of it. Sitting with me in my therapy office, Kyra had seemed confused. This loneliness would just not leave her alone. It was not what she expected from her three-year-old marriage. In their wedding vows, her soon-to-be husband had promised to have and to hold her, but she was feeling let down.

"If this were a good relationship," she pondered, "I would not be feeling this way." But it was hard for me to see how the marriage could be much better, without completely changing the characters of the husband and wife.

"I just don't want to feel 'second,'" Kyra had said, as she told me how upset she got when her husband interrupted her carefully prepared dinner to take a phone call from his cousin. It reminded her of how she used to feel when she was a child and her mother and sister would talk animatedly with each other. She would tug on her mother's sleeve with a question but still be ignored. She thought those feelings were behind her—she had found the man she loved and he was her friend as well as her lover.

"Maybe he's not man enough to really come after me," she wondered aloud, sounding a bit apologetic, aware of how "retro" this idea might sound to me.

While I was sympathetic to Kyra's needs for intimacy, I felt there was something unrealistic in her demands. She seemed to be having an experience of loneliness that is quite widespread among people who, in one way or another, "have everything." Most of us are brought up to think that the key to happiness lies outside of ourselves. We look forward to falling in love, having a family, making a career, or building a home, and expect that those levels of accomplishment will be enough. But often we find, to our own chagrin, that when one level of need is satisfied, another stands ready to take its place.

There are a variety of reactions when these new needs assert themselves. The most common, as Kyra discovered, is to try to squeeze more juice out of what one already has. She wanted *more* time, *more* sex, and her husband to be *more* of a man. She was still directing everything at him. Another common strategy is to try to override the feelings of loneliness with behaviors that have worked previously to alleviate it. So people turn to food, drugs or alcohol, or to secret attempts at sexual gratification to try to drown out their disappointment. This is the path of compulsion or addiction, and its casualties are legion. The third, and related, reaction, is to begin to turn against that which one also needs. Kyra was dangerously close to that already. Once she was unable to get her husband to give her more attention, she began attacking him, first in her thoughts and then in her actions. She would withdraw, become sullen and disparage him sexually, contaminating their intimate relations and closing herself off. Then she would feel more justified in her unhappiness. Should this dynamic proceed unchecked, I had no doubt that Kyra's marriage would fracture, freeing her to seek happiness through the attention of another man. But Kyra could face the same predicament somewhere down the road.

The dawning of loneliness is a very strange time in a relationship. Sometimes it is a sign that something is clearly wrong, and that action must be taken to set things back on course. But this is not always the case. It is one of the age-old truths about love that, while it offers unparalleled opportunities for union and the lifting of ego boundaries, at the same time it washes us up on the shores of the loved one's otherness. Sooner or later, as Sita and Rama demonstrated in the *Ramayana*, and as I was playing out in my pursuit of the lobster roll, love makes us feel inescapably separate.

Most psychological experts counsel a certain level of resignation in the face of this disappointment. Some desires, like the one for total intimacy, can never be met, the experts remind us. Freud was notorious is his promulgation of the "reality principle," in which insistent demands for pleasure have to give way to the truth of limitation and restriction. He saw the task of therapy as helping people move from a place of neurotic misery to one of common unhappiness, and, for him, that was movement enough. One psychoanalyst who has contemplated the contradictory nature of love, however, has come up with a more hopeful formulation. "Love," wrote Otto Kernberg, who has devoted the better part of his long career to the study of intimate human relations, "is the revelation of the other person's freedom."[1]

The implication of Kernberg's statement is that there is a spiritual dimension to this residue of loneliness. In the revelation of another person's freedom is a window into a state of non-clinging. This is the state that the Buddha proclaimed as the "good news" of his Third Noble Truth. While desire yearns for completion, and seeks it most commonly in love, it can find the freedom it is looking for only by not clinging.

One of my earliest spiritual teachers, Jack Kornfield, tells a very interesting story about his own battles with loneliness while training as a monk in Thailand.[2] While the forsaken feelings of a young monk in a foreign monastery might seem a far cry from the pangs of yearning in an intimate relationship, they actually have much in common. For a long time in his solitary meditations, Jack was besieged by sexual longing. Embarrassed by the compulsive nature of his thoughts and fantasies, Jack finally began to discuss his predicament with his elderly Thai teacher.

"What should I do with all this?" he asked, and he was surprised to hear the old man tell him to simply observe his longings. He worked hard at that, applying what is called "bare," or nonjudgmental, attention to whatever he was experiencing. All manner of sexual material continued to fill his mind. But slowly, feelings of loneliness began to emerge. His lust was not only lust, but a way of seeking closeness and comfort.

In most cases, this revelation would have been enough, but because Jack was engaged in a long-term retreat, he continued to observe his inner process. Much as Kyra discovered in her therapy, Jack's loneliness seemed tied to an early childhood feeling of insufficiency.

"There is something wrong with me and I will always be rejected," he found himself thinking. He knew this to be a core belief about himself, but instead of closing down around it with self-pity, he opened to it in the spirit of acceptance. Slowly but surely, the hungry yearning yielded to a feeling of spaciousness that filled and lightened his heart. Disturbing emptiness gave way to clear space. His identity as a lonely person unworthy of love shifted into something much more open and undefined.

The feelings persisted, but they were stripped of the quality of "poor me." His cravings receded as the possibility of non-clinging became clearer.

Jack's revelations while meditating in the Thai monastery were spurred on by a very important insight, one that Buddhism always stresses in its approach to alleviating suffering. By observing his mind so closely, Jack zeroed in on a central self-image that was unconsciously ruling him. "There is something wrong with me and I will always be rejected," he found himself thinking. This core belief about himself was structuring much of his experience of the world. It was his own self that felt flawed, and much of his eroticized desire was prompted by a wish to make this imperfect self disappear. Once he could see that there was nothing *ultimately* real about this particular view of himself, it began to lose its central dominance in his psyche. The experience of such a core belief dissolving into clear space freed him of a burden that he had been carrying since childhood. The Buddha taught that all self-images are empty in this way and that the residual loneliness that we feel even in the midst of love is caused by attachment to these self-representations.

Kyra did not yet have the meditative intensity of Jack's self-awareness to help her, but she was able to head down the same path. In her talks with me, she could see that she was an expert in closeness, having learned how to weave herself into someone else's space in order to make them happy.

"I know how to put them first," she told me proudly, with a trace of exasperation at her husband's inability to do the same for her.

"You don't want to feel second, yet you always put the other person first," I pointed out.

Kyra admitted that she had never thought of it that way before and then had as close to a breakthrough as happens in psychotherapy.

"The loneliness is being close to myself," she said softly, her eyes opening wide in trepidation.

THE END OF THE OBJECT

Kyra's revelation was important because it stopped her from turning desire into a descending spiral of disappointment, frustration, anger and destruction. It broke the connection between loneliness and low self-esteem that began years ago when she struggled unsuccessfully for her mother's attention. Like Jack, Kyra had, in her heart, taken her loneliness to mean that she was flawed. By staying with the feeling a little longer, instead of rushing to an old judgment about it, she opened up other possible meanings. In recognizing that her loneliness meant being close to herself, Kyra began to explore what the Buddha meant when he taught the emptiness of self. Being close to ourselves is frightening when we are always trying to be something more than we are. In letting go of the specific negativity that was associated with her mother's lack of attention, Kyra was able to work out a more honest relationship with her self, one in which she was less sure about who she was or what was wrong with her. Rather than affirming a deep well of negativity, this willingness to face her loneliness began to give her strength. It opened up her inner life. She felt herself reaching out for her husband from the lonely place instead of cowering in it. And she found that her love for him did not have to be directly proportional to the attention he gave her. Although it went against much of the way she thought about relationships, there was something exciting in this. An aloneness uncontaminated with self-pity could be very fertile.

As my thoughts circled these conversations with Kyra, my experience with the lobster roll suddenly took on a new meaning. I realized, with some embarrassment, that it read like a metaphor for an affair. When the first moment of freedom had opened up earlier that afternoon, my impulse had been to turn to my wife. I was actually after something much more consuming than lunch—that spark of connection that I knew was possible in my marriage but that was temporarily unavailable because of my wife's obligations to her studio. The lobster roll was a kind of substitute, although I do not think she will appreciate the comparison. But again, by trying to find a substitute, I was privileging the external direction over the internal. I was reluctant to stay within myself. The disappointment that I felt may have had to do with the impossibility of fulfilling any kind of sensory desire, but it also seemed to me suddenly to be a message about the ultimate futility of trying to erase the feelings of loneliness that mask an insecure self. As the Buddha taught, there is no better time to understand "no-self" than when we are feeling most insecure.

Reflecting about an affair put me in mind of another bit of Indian religious history. Sometime in the early seventeen hundreds in India there were great religious debates about which kind of passion was more sublime, that between married couples or that which was adulterous. The debates were indicative of the esteem that desire was then afforded in certain religious circles, an esteem that has deep roots on the Indian subcontinent. Adulterous desire won out, because it was understood that the highest passion, "divine desire," depends on what was called the "flavor of separation." Marriage in those days meant ownership of the wife by the husband, and there was not room, in that kind of domestic arrangement, for couples to stay enough out of each other's reach for there to be the kind of tantalizing longing that makes passion passionate. Husband and wife were too conscious of their roles for there to be enough of a quality of unpredictability between them. It was all too scripted. The divine spark depends on otherness, the sages divined, but in that time and place otherness was possible only under the umbrella of the illicit.

It is different now. In today's world, if we are lucky, we have relationships between two subjects, not between owner and object. My marriage was not like one from medieval India, where my wife was my property and where her desire was irrelevant to my satisfaction. It was of a different ilk, more like that which the Indian sages saw as adulterous. We were two individuals, with completely different subjective experiences, who could not always be together, but who secretly thrilled when we managed to find each other. My work during this time, my *yoga*, was to remember this. I had to differentiate my "hungry" desire from my true longing, and be patient. To the extent that I could not tolerate my frustration, I was destined to repeat the lobster roll experience. But to the extent that I could appreciate the flavor of separation, I maintained the possibility of a resurgent fulfillment.

As Kyra discovered, and as I needed to be reminded, the loneliness that exists in love relationships, the flavor of separation, is grist for the mill on the path of desire. It is the means of deepening one's understanding of self and one's appreciation of the other, what is called *subjectivity* in today's psychological language. Desire deepens subjectivity precisely because it can never be totally assuaged. It leaves us with ourselves, as well as granting freedom to our lovers. From a Buddhist perspective, this is a wonderful outcome. The self that we are left with is exactly what the Buddha wants us to explore. We might think that it is flawed, but it is the source of as much potential as the love we seek. As much as I might chafe against this, I could see that the flavor of separation was what kept relationships vital. It allowed for a taste that I could savor, a taste that came from both within and without, a taste worth cultivating: one that spoke to the possibility of working creatively, rather than addictively, with desire. It certainly beat the lobster roll.

5

The Backward Glance

In the *Ramayana*, each of the four principal characters represents a different face of desire. Ravana is the embodiment of
clinging, grasping after the perfect moment, objectifying his
beloved with a relentless insistence that drives her away. Hanuman is the liminal figure, the one who goes between each of the
others and makes the gap between lover and beloved more tolerable. He is the representation of the inner life that develops in
response to limitation and frustration. Sita is the personal voice
that develops out of this inner life. Her task is to stay true to her
deepest longings. Hanuman is there to help her, but she must
still find and sustain her own truth. Rama, as the incarnation of
God, represents desire without clinging, but even he must fight
a huge battle in order to discover his true nature.

The first great task of the path of desire, as exemplified by the *Ramayana*, is to enter willingly into the gap that desire brings. The second important task is to honestly confront the manifestations of clinging as they arise in all aspects of life. It is not enough to understand the problem intellectually or to reach for the alternative spiritually. Over and over again, clinging must be identified as it arises and seen clearly for what it is. Any attempt to justify it must be confronted. In classical meditation, this is often attempted through moment-to-moment microscopic observation of thoughts and feelings. On this micro level one tries to observe clinging as it arises in the mind. If a pleasant feeling or a happy memory arises, for example, it is often possible to observe ourselves hanging on to the feeling or memory after it has already passed. We just do not want to let it go. We can see, in this activity, the trace or reflection of a young child who does not want his parents to go out the door. If an unpleasant thought or feeling arises, we can observe a parallel tendency: an instinctive unwillingness or refusal to admit the material into our consciousness, even though we have no real choice in the matter. We are like children who refuse to look the babysitter in the eye.

The path of desire demands this same level of honest self-scrutiny in our intimate and relational lives. While classical meditation focuses on the micro level, the left-handed path dwells on the macro. The attempt is to catch the obstacles, called "fixations" in Buddhist philosophy, that reduce desire to the level of clinging in our daily lives. In this light, psychotherapy can be an invaluable resource, since its observational field, unlike classical meditation, is the world of human relationship. As therapists have discovered, we tend to chase satisfaction, turning toward that which provided it in the past, instead of learning to work with the separation inherent in the process of desiring. Drugs, alcohol, sex, food, shopping, flirtations, pornography and gambling are just some of the things that we can attach ourselves to in the attempt to evade the fault that desire tends to open, but these are just the grossest of the fixations. On an emotional level, the fixations that cause clinging usually have to do with an insistence that another person meet all of our expectations.

In Buddhist psychology, the root cause of fixation is the assumption of "thingness" in persons or objects that, from a Buddhist way of thinking, have no inherent, or ultimate, identity. It is the mind's tendency to become obsessed with this "thingness," to see sources of pleasure as more real than they actually are and to chase them with a proliferation of thoughts and feelings. In the *Ramayana*, Ravana is the most literal representation of this tendency. His mind is obsessed with possession of Sita, a control that is imagined to be possible precisely because of the way he objectifies her. But this concretization of reality is a mistake. People are not objects, and, in the Buddhist way of thinking, even objects are not objects. People and things do not exist in and of themselves in any kind of lasting way. They are all ultimately impermanent, insubstantial and, if we are not very careful, disappointing. When we try to control them, so that they will meet our needs, they tend to rebel.

Desire, as we have seen, springs from a place of incompleteness. It is a natural reaction to the human predicament. No one, after all, is self-sufficient. In searching outside of ourselves for wholeness, however, we set ourselves up for clinging. We assume that solutions all lie in the external: that if we can just be united with *that person* or *this thing* that we will be complete, our problems over. Aristophanes, in a parable quoted by Plato and resurrected by Freud, assumed that we were all descended from hermaphroditic ancestors who were cut in half by Zeus. Ever seeking our lost other half, we spend our lives trying to resurrect a lost unity,[1] searching for a wholeness, or union, that might bring us back to ourselves. This is a dangerous fantasy because it overempowers the object of desire, setting it up as capable of providing a satisfaction that is not in its nature. The path of desire requires something more (or something less) than an imagined unity with the beloved.

HUNGRY GHOSTS

In the Buddhist world, this longing for an imagined wholeness is portrayed in what is called the Six Realms of Existence, an age-old method of conceptualizing psychic reality that is a very compelling Eastern model of the mind. The Six Realms are often described visually in the form of a popular motif called the Wheel of Life, or the Wheel of Desire. Used originally as a visual diagram of the various realms through which a sentient being might take birth, the *mandala*, or circle, is also a penetrating description of all the ways the mind tries to deal with the gap that desire creates. It is a map of the mind states that we pass through as we grapple with the dissatisfaction that is endemic to our predicament, a description of all the possible permutations of desire. One of the Six Realms is that of the Hungry Ghosts, beings who are in a state of chronic deprivation and longing, always searching for a nourishment that they are not equipped to digest.

Hungry Ghosts haunt the offices of psychotherapists. They were the ones who taught Freud the meaning of *transference*, the process by which the traumas of old, unfinished relationships are reexperienced in new ones. In the Buddhist cosmology, Hungry Ghosts have a very peculiar anatomy. Although they seek nourishment, their mucous membranes are stretched so thin that even the touch of water is painful to their mouths and lips. They remind me of the way I felt in Jamaica, when the medicine I took to help me feel closer to my wife turned my skin to sandpaper. The Hungry Ghosts have long thin necks and grossly bloated bellies, like pictures of starving children that we see in the newspapers. The act of swallowing is intensely painful.

The most disturbing aspect of the Hungry Ghost psychology is that no satisfaction is possible. Their attempts at gratification just make them hungrier and thirstier. Often, people come to psychotherapy in the grip of a Hungry Ghost. This is a wonderful opportunity, painful though it might seem, to gain insight into the latent wisdom of desire. These scenarios are always driven by clinging, and when they create enough of a crisis, it becomes possible to learn how to relax one's grip.

A patient of mine named Philip, for instance, a wildly successful criminal lawyer in his late forties, found all kinds of things to talk to me about before raising the specter of his Hungry Ghost. Philip was married to a beautiful woman whom he spoke about in admiring tones. They had two children and a life together that he seemed legitimately to treasure. But when Philip traveled for business, which he did on a fairly regular basis, his sexual appetite would become aroused. What began with an occasional adult movie in his hotel room turned, over the years, into a more involved foray into the world of sex for hire.

Philip liked treating himself to an erotic massage when he

was away from home. He worked hard on his cases and then would retreat to his hotel, where he would arrange his clandestine visits late in the evening. For a long time he told himself that there was nothing to be ashamed of in this routine. While he did not tell his wife about it, he did not think of it as cheating. A pragmatic man, Philip saw his exploits mainly in pragmatic terms. He worked hard and wanted a release, and this was much more pleasurable than masturbation. Philip enjoyed the pure sensuality of the massage, and he found that if he took a little bit of Viagra before it began that he enjoyed it even more. The Viagra allowed his erection to blossom without his having to worry about it and permitted an exquisite period of erotic anticipation while he waited for his masseuse to take notice.

Lately, on his business trips, Philip had begun exploring "harmless" sadomasochistic rituals with several young women who seemed happy to indulge his fantasies in return for his money. He particularly enjoyed having his hands bound and being forced to plead, or, in his words, "grovel," for his lover's physical attention. A little prohibition seemed to work just as well as the Viagra for him. After a long day of being in charge of so many things, Philip found it very liberating to give himself over to another's power, especially if the final control rested with him. But Philip was a little disturbed at how compulsive his behavior was becoming. What had begun as a sidelight, or a special treat, was fast becoming the central thing in his mind. He was traveling more, and working less, rushing back to his hotel rooms for longer and longer trysts. The scenarios that he was acting out were becoming more and more convoluted and time-consuming. He had become attached to several of his sexual partners and was worried that people might start to talk and that his wife might somehow discover his activities. And he was spending a lot of money.

Philip's agenda for therapy, once he began to discuss the details of his extracurricular sexual activities, was for the confession to cure him of his behavior. When it did not, he began to despair. He painted a picture of himself as helpless to react differently when given the opportunity to indulge his fantasies. Despite his guilt and his fears, he could not resist when the moment opened up. In a confession that is very common to people struggling with clinging, he found that once he opened the door a tiny bit, he inevitably lost control.

My first inquiries had to do with his sexual relationship with his wife. Other things were more important, he noted. Especially the children. Sex with her was fine, but not exciting in the same way. He offered only a few details. His wife was reluctant to give him oral sex when he asked for it. She turned away from him quickly when they were finished making love. She did not have a lot of time for him.

What would happen if he brought a little of the illicit activity into his erotic relationship with her, I wondered? Why such a split between his activities apart from her and his behavior in her presence? She wouldn't be interested, he was sure. She would think it was immature. He did not want to reveal himself in that way to her. This was not a good suggestion, he was clear about that.

Stymied, I took a different tack. What if he tried to bring more self-awareness to those moments in the hotel *before* he made his first telephone call? He felt himself to be helpless, but maybe he could find the wherewithal to react differently when faced with so much freedom, and so much aloneness. Could he pay attention to his emotional experience at those times? Was it purely a physical desire that he was trying to satisfy, or was there some other kind of longing that he could pay attention to, perhaps find gratification for in a different way? I thought that perhaps Philip's behavior was masking some kind of emotional need that he was relatively unaware of, perhaps a difficulty being by himself. Maybe he could discover something by coming close to the behavior but staying with the need, rather than rushing to have it satisfied. Philip liked this suggestion better than my last one. It drew from a shared interest in meditation, and demanded that he bring awareness to times that he was certainly not thinking of as meditative. But it proved to be equally unhelpful. Philip did not find anything of more interest in those moments than excitement and desire. He still found himself powerless to resist.

I must point out that Philip's plight had elicited from me a response that was not in keeping with the usual stance of a psychodynamic therapist. He was a practical man and he was looking for practical suggestions from me, more along the lines of what a cognitive or behavioral therapist might offer. He did not want to "waste time" in therapy and I was drawn into his agenda. I never got to explore his anger at his wife or the ways that his frustration and disappointment with her played into his extracurricular sexual activities. Nor did we talk much about his overriding need for affirmation and attention, his difficulties being alone without some kind of erotic stimulation to feed or comfort him. Instead, I tried to help him find ways to accomplish his goal, while still being respectful of whatever his sexual choices actually were. But none of these efforts bore much fruit. Philip stopped coming regularly and faded from my consciousness.

Some time later, I got a call from him out of the blue. He

just wanted to let me know, he told me, that he had gone for an interview with a visiting spiritual teacher from India. He had told her about his problem and she had instructed him, in no uncertain terms, to cease all such behavior. No pornography, no massage, no extracurricular relationships. She asked him to take a vow, similar to what is called *brahmacharya*, or celibacy, in Hinduism, to restrict his sexual life to his relationship with his wife. He had agreed, and he was marveling at what relief he was feeling. Instead of submitting to his dominatrix, Philip had surrendered to his guru. He seemed to have broken the cycle of lust, guilt and self-loathing that had brought him to me in the first place. While I had wondered if my practical suggestions might have been straying too far from therapeutic neutrality, it turned out that my suggestions were not practical enough! Philip needed to be told to stop, and he was ready to listen to this kind of counsel.

I have no way of knowing whether Philip's transformation was sustained or short-lived. I never heard from him again. There are certainly plenty of stories about people making such vows, like adolescent attempts to stop masturbating, only to succumb again and again. Most therapists, I assume, would be suspicious of a story like Philip's. But there was something in his tone that gave me pause. He sounded like someone who finds help in Alcoholics Anonymous after trying any number of other approaches to stop drinking. The daily vow of abstinence, backed by an ethical motivation and, in the case of the 12-step programs, the shared support of a community, can effectively counter the obsessional dead ends that we know as addiction. It seemed to be the best way for Philip to gain a little space in his mind from the compulsive activity that his sexual forays had become.

ABSTINENCE

Another patient, a talented twenty-nine-year-old dancer named Juliet, came to me in the midst of an affair with the man who had choreographed her last performance. He was a respected director, a man well connected in the dance and theater world whom she admired greatly, and someone whom she was already having major fantasies about sharing a life with. Having worked so intimately together on their last piece, they shared an aesthetic that had immediate positive reverberations when they slept together. In sex with him, she was known, and touched, in a way that reached to her soul, but he was not calling her back after sleeping with her. Weeks had gone by, and he had already broken several promises about when he would talk to her next. She was confused by his disappearance and was casting about for explanations.

This pattern continued for the next year. Brief rendezvous followed by long periods of silence. Hours of therapy spent trying to make sense of the contradictory nature of the relationship. A faith, slowly eroded, in the power of love to conquer all obstacles. An emerging realization that he must have a problem with alcohol. As with Philip, most of my attempts to change Juliet's perspective on her situation came up short. She had a hard time accepting that her lover did not value their connection as much as she did. It was confusing for both of us because I did not feel that she was exaggerating how intense it was between them.

Juliet was not in as much of a hurry as Philip had been to finish therapy, and our conversations led to some interesting discussions about her father's boundary problems with her when she was young, and her subsequent aversion to him and to a man's dependent feelings. This aversion seemed to lead her into relationships with men like her director who were constantly evading her. Such boyfriends retained their power to attract, and their mystery, while never making themselves too vulnerable. But this left Juliet yearning for a mutuality that was never forthcoming.

My most effective intervention came one afternoon when I blurted out suddenly, after Juliet was bemoaning the love that she felt between them, "He doesn't love you. Is this how *you* would treat someone you loved?" We were both taken aback. It is rare for a therapist to be so declarative, but I had the trust in her to let myself say it. How could I really know if he loved her or not? Wasn't *I* overstepping my boundaries now?

But Juliet had a reaction that was similar to Philip's response to his guru. It did not come right away, but she brought my response up again a few weeks later. "I keep hearing you saying that he doesn't love me and it makes me laugh," she said tearfully. "You sounded so sure." Somehow my reaction allowed Juliet a little more flexibility. The relationship began to seem like an addiction to her, rather than a love affair. So preoccupied had she become that Juliet's life energy was completely monopolized. Her devotion to her lover was inspiring but her judgment was not. Her only choice, she began to realize, was to renounce him.

In psychoanalysis, the root cause of the insatiable craving of the Hungry Ghosts is usually given a more psychological basis than in the Buddhist world. Early trauma, whether in the form of parental intrusiveness or parental abandonment, sets up a yearning for a relationship that can never be, while simultaneously driving people to reproduce their traumatizing relationships, replaying them over and over again in new interactions with lovers, teachers, therapists and friends. When early relationships with parents are *not* traumatizing, what develops is a capacity for attachment that makes room for separation. This non-traumatizing interaction is called a "facilitating environment" by the British child therapist D. W. Winnicott. What it facilitates is the ability to negotiate disappointment, something that meditation provides a second chance to consolidate.

But the Hungry Ghosts have not reached this stage of development. They are motivated by a deprivation that, in most cases, has not been accepted, digested or metabolized. They tend to feel flawed or broken, unworthy of love and, as one of my patients recently put it, "subhuman." As children tend to do, they take too much responsibility for what they are feeling, blaming themselves instead of understanding that the roots of their difficult feelings lie in traumas that have already happened. In the place of really experiencing the pain of their childhood loneliness, they obsessively seek nourishment from people and things who can only disappoint, repeating the trauma instead of working it through. That is why renunciation is so important in the Hungry Ghost Realm, why it was the only intervention that worked for Philip and Juliet. Renunciation of clinging is the first step in grieving the pain of the past, the prerequisite for forgiveness and a more unfettered desire.

In the Wheel of Life, this knowledge is encoded in the form of the Bodhisattva of Compassion, who appears, as a tiny figure, in each of the Realms dressed in a different costume, symbolic of the understanding that is necessary to free oneself from the bonds of that particular fixation. In the Hungry Ghost Realm, he is cloaked in the garments of the renouncer, carrying objects symbolic of spiritual nourishment. He knows what the psychoanalyst has also discovered: The gratification that the Hungry

Ghost seeks cannot be found in the form in which it is imagined. Only when that drive is forsaken can the real work begin.

The desire to know oneself more deeply is often rooted in the feeling of never having been known. This is not a new phenomenon, nor one that is restricted to the modern nuclear family structure. I remember a story from the life of the Buddha that always interested me. Even in his time, twenty-five hundred years ago, relations between parents and children were problematic. After his enlightenment, and several years into his wandering and teaching, the Buddha returned to his hometown of Kapilavatthu to be received by his father, uncles and cousins. It is noteworthy that it took him several years to return to the town of his youth; perhaps he needed some time before he could confront his past. Well-known for their pride and limited by the rules of interaction that prohibited elders from paying respect to their juniors, his relatives were disinclined to pay homage to him.

"Who does he think he is?" I imagine them thinking. "A Buddha?"

Rather than getting angry, the Buddha created something of a fireworks display. Like many of my patients who struggle with the feelings of never being seen, he, too, needed to impress. In an event called the Twin Marvel,[2] he suddenly radiated jets of fire and water from all of his limbs. It took a miracle to get his relatives' attention. His father still took criticism from his clan for bowing down to the Buddha in the aftermath of this performance; it was thought unseemly for a father to bow to a son in those times.

"I bow not to my son, but to the Lord of gods and humans," he is said to have responded, in an effort to justify his actions to his tradition-bound kinsmen.

In the rapprochement that followed, the Buddha's father, King Shuddhodhana, made one request of his son. He took the opening that the magical display created and used it to express some of his pent-up feelings. It was painful to have lost his son to the dharma, the king confessed, now he was about to lose his grandson and several others of the clan, newly inspired by the Buddha's visit. Could the Buddha not make a rule that would require parental consent before one could join the community of monks? The Buddha agreed. He did not want joining the order to become a vehicle of adolescent rebellion, another manifestation of the clinging he was trying to undo.

Although we might think that the strategy of renunciation is rooted only in the spiritual traditions of the world's religions, it is also fundamental to the successful practice of any form of psychotherapy. There can be no treatment without an extraordinary amount of abstinence on the part of both therapist and patient. This is one of the ways that psychotherapy functions as a stepping-stone on the left-handed path. The therapist, by not gratifying, but not rejecting, the unfinished cravings of the Hungry Ghosts, models a new approach to desire. By examining those cravings in the nonjudgmental space of the therapeutic encounter, the therapist encourages a renunciation, not of desire itself, but of the clinging that comes to obscure it. Despite the Buddha's need to impress his kinsmen, this capacity to renounce clinging is, from a Buddhist perspective, thought to be miracle enough.

6

Renunciation

In a recent discussion with Western psychologists on the managing of destructive emotions like anger, greed and envy, the Dalai Lama was asked by one of the participants if there were any emotions that he could think of that might preserve or reinforce the calmness of mind that he thought was so important, and so lacking in today's world. The question came somewhat out of frustration. The way the Dalai Lama had been talking about emotional experience, it was starting to seem as if he saw all emotions as afflictive. This was puzzling to many of the Western participants, who seemed more likely than their Tibetan counterparts to give value to their emotional lives. Were there no positive aspects of emotional life that the Dalai Lama could think of?

His answer was very interesting.

"Renunciation," he replied, is an emotion that can contribute to peace of mind. "It is the first step to really, thoroughly determining how vulnerable we are to suffering. If we understand how utterly vulnerable we are, and recognize that these mental afflictions make us so vulnerable, then we can see the possibility of the mind becoming free of those mental afflictions."

It was difficult for the Westerners at this meeting to conceive of renunciation as an emotion until the translator for the Dalai Lama, an American scholar named Alan Wallace, gave an etymological clarification. The Tibetan word that the Dalai Lama used to describe the "emotion" of renunciation could more literally be translated as "a spirit of emergence." Rather than renunciation being something that we impose on ourselves, as the Western mind, steeped in Protestantism and the Freudian superego, tends to conceive it, it can be something that emerges out of self-awareness. The Dalai Lama described it in more detail for his listeners.

"You are recognizing the nature of suffering, but you also sense the possibility of emerging from this ubiquitous vulnerability to suffering—this is why it is called the spirit of emergence. The spirit of emergence could also be called an emotion; there is an enormous amount of emotional content to it. It entails a radical disillusionment with the whole of *samsara*. And so, whether you call it disgust or disillusionment, it is a profound sadness with respect to the mundane. This is all, theoretically, in anticipation of ascertaining the possibility of nirvana—complete and irreversible freedom from mental afflictions."[1]

In the Dalai Lama's comments, we can hear the echo of the Buddha's Four Noble Truths and the wisdom encoded in the Tibetan mandala of the Wheel of Life. We can also still hear the whisper of desire. The first two critical tasks of the left-handed path reveal themselves in his explication: the willingness to look at the gap that desire creates—what the Dalai Lama called "the nature of suffering"—and the ability to see the clinging that results—what he called the "sadness with respect to the mundane."

Out of these insights comes a feeling, not of resignation or depression (as we might expect), but of hope. A new emotion, in the Dalai Lama's lexicon, can be found.

A SPIRIT OF EMERGENCE

This is the third critical task of the left-handed path: Renunciation need not mean a turning away from desire, but only a forsaking of the acting out that clinging creates. In the Dalai Lama's formulation, there is a different view of renunciation than the self-punitive one that usually comes to mind when the concept is invoked.

In his use of the term "disillusionment" there are traces of what we in the West would more clearly call "mourning" or "grieving." The profound sadness that the Dalai Lama referred to is a weariness at the impossibility of desire's demands. How much shopping can we do, how many sexual experiences can we have, how much food can we eat before we have to admit that we are not getting what we are looking for? In psychological terms, we could say that so much desire is trapped in the vain attempt to get what we never had as children that we do not even know where our desire can actually take us. But the turning away that the Dalai Lama envisions is more than just a turning away from the past, it is also a turning away from an entire approach to life, one that could be called completion by consumption. In this approach, the self is felt to be in competition with every other self for the scarce resources necessary for survival. We could call it a Darwinian approach, in which survival of the fittest is the ruling tendency of the mind. The renunciation that emerges when we start to recognize the limitations of this tendency allows for the growth of empathy and compassion. There is a strange sense of no longer being the center of the universe.

I saw an example of this in my office the other day. A woman whom I have been seeing in therapy on and off for many years needed to talk with me. A former artist now running her own public relations firm, Bonnie was a hardworking businesswoman stressed by the demands of her ever expanding work life. Divorced and in her late forties, she had a tendency toward a kind of self-pitying anger that erupted whenever she felt shortchanged, by a business associate, employee, family member or lover. This was a tendency that I had noted for years but had never really been able to do much about. I tended to sympathize with her at such times, as she was usually correct in feeling somewhat taken advantage of, manipulated or mistreated, but my sympathies always felt a bit like Band-Aids that never really confronted the deeper issues, whatever they might be. In the midst of a story about an employee who had left suddenly for a better job, leaving Bonnie hassled and in the lurch, I suddenly registered an "entitled" quality to her anger that I had never quite focused on before. She was engaged in a bit of a rant. My highlighting of this quality brought about a shift in Bonnie's mood. In the place of what had begun to resemble a self-pitying harangue, Bonnie began to talk about how the quality that I was noticing went back a very long way:

"It's what makes me eat compulsively," she said, in what seemed at first like something of a non sequitur, "and not take care of myself very well. Sometimes I just close the door on everything and everyone and eat until I feel sick."

While Bonnie had told me one or two stories over the years about being in hotel rooms on business trips and eating the candy in minibars, she had never talked to me about how extensively she used food to try to manage her feelings. As she began to talk about it now, she remembered back to her childhood.

"I can remember where those feelings first came from," she told me. "I've told you about this before. I was sitting on the stairs outside my mother's bedroom. My mother was dressed in what I called her 'Franciscan robe,' a brown bathrobe wrapped with a cord, and she was lying on her bed with her arms crossed on her chest. She lay there for days."

Bonnie's mother was prone to depression, and had tried to kill herself several times. She would sometimes go for days without coming out of her room, leaving Bonnie to sit outside the bedroom wondering if she had done something to hurt her. We talked, for the first time, about the deprivation that Bonnie had endured, about her submerged sadness and rage, and about the feelings of being damaged that inevitably accompany such deprivation. Bonnie could remember "closing the door" on feeling deprived, making up stories about how happy she was in her family to present to the outside world, cultivating a cheery persona that led to much professional success. But Bonnie was also aware, in our discussion, of how much she had always wanted to get rid of the bad feelings, to eradicate the deprivation that went so deep in her experience. For many years she had longed for a relationship that would remove those feelings, but this had not worked out for her. Now she was secretly eating (behind closed doors) in a similar attempt to banish, or overwhelm, the deprivation.

I could see that Bonnie was playing out something very close to what the Buddha had warned about twenty-five hundred years before. In an effort to avoid the pain of her reality, Bonnie was resorting to one of desire's fixations. Instead of seeing her situation clearly and processing the traumas that had befallen her, she was succumbing to the lure of craving. Each of her attempts to deal with her emotional state involved trying, in one form or another, to quell uncomfortable feelings. When she was young, Bonnie had simply suppressed her pain—later in life she tried to drown it out with food or with relationships. One approach she had not yet tried was the Buddhist one. Having become aware of the connection between eating and her un-worked-through emotional trauma, Bonnie was now on the verge of being able to renounce her self-destructive behaviors from a place of self-understanding, rather than self-punishment. This is the crucial distinction that the Dalai Lama was getting at in his talk with the Western therapists: When renunciation arises out of self-awareness, its function is not to dampen desire but to liberate it.

For Bonnie, desire had always been about wanting what she never had enough of, consumption in search of completion. In acknowledging her pain, and renouncing her attempts to eliminate it, Bonnie changed a long-standing dynamic in which she was always weighing how much she gave against what she received. She stopped fighting with her feelings of incompleteness. Relieved of this burden, Bonnie's bitterness began to fade. In its place came a simpler kind of caring, a generosity beyond anything she had ever known.

TAPAS AND KAMA

This understanding of the interrelationship of abstinence, or renunciation, and empathy has a very clear foundation in the Indian spiritual traditions. Restraining the actions provoked by clinging allows desire to function in a new way. Restraint brings about a restructuring of subjective experience. Rather than compulsively seeking satisfactions that can only eventually disappoint, restraint keeps people closer to their emotional vulnerabilities. As the Dalai Lama pointed out, this can be sad, but ultimately a relief.

The psychoanalytic world also has a tradition that recognizes the interrelationship of renunciation and desire. There is a saying in psychotherapy, growing out of the work of D. W. Winnicott, that at the center of each person is what is called an *incommunicado element*, an isolation that is impossible to breach, a matrix of emotional experience that can never be fully communicated. Winnicott's descriptions of the incommunicado element were moving because of the way in which he fearlessly refered to it as sacred. In psychoanalysis, to refer to anything as sacred is virtually taboo. But Winnicott recognized what happens all too often to children like my patient Bonnie. Cut off from themselves because of the traumas that unfold in their early lives, they learn to put on a mask in order to cope with the demands of their worlds. They do this to survive, but lose touch with the vast, vulnerable potential that was their birthright. To be cut off from one's self like this is to set up a scenario of clinging, as exemplified by the Hungry Ghosts. Bonnie did not know that she was cut off from herself, she just knew that she did not feel good. She wanted to feel better and turned to whatever she could think of: food, relationships or therapy. But Winnicott, in his writings on the sacredness of the incommunicado element, knew something that the Dalai Lama and the whole tradition of Indian spirituality also understand: In order to feel better, she had to learn how to go within.

Sometimes, the subtlety of the renunciation required by the path of desire can be surprising. The acting out provoked by clinging does not always take the form of addictive behaviors—it often is restricted to compulsive thoughts. But the consequences are the same—a person so afflicted is handcuffed by these reactions. Desire is so restricted that the spirit of emergence cannot be born.

A patient of mine, a painter in her early thirties named Amanda, discovered a version of this at a recent meditation retreat. Amanda was an accomplished yoga student who had a natural ease with meditation. She could sit serenely in the meditation hall for hours without moving and exhibited a grace that was the envy of many of her peers. At this retreat, a ten-day silent Buddhist exercise in mindfulness, in which an effort is made to attend to whatever is happening in the mind and body throughout the day in the style originally taught by the Buddha, Amanda was taught a technique of noting, or labeling, whatever she was aware of. When breathing in, she would say "in" to herself, when breathing out, she would say "out." When discomfort arose, she would note "pain," and when irritation arose, she would note "anger." This is the traditional means of practicing *vipassana*, or "insight" meditation, and, as is often the case, after several days, Amanda's mind became much more peaceful and calm. She began to have long, extended, and quite pleasurable fantasies about falling in love, raising a family and being with a man in whom she delighted, and she passed many hours of meditation immersed in these thoughts. A quiet joy permeated her being throughout this time.

As is the custom at these retreats, every other day Amanda would go to one of the teachers for a ten- to fifteen-minute interview. In one of these sessions, with the teacher Joseph Goldstein, Amanda was asked to describe the moment-to-moment contents of a recent meditation. She told Joseph, with a touch of pride, about the fantasies in which she was dwelling, half expecting that he would commend her for the loving state of mind she had discovered.

"Do you know what the label for that is?" he asked her.

She shook her head mutely.

"Dead end," he said.

Amanda was shocked by Joseph's intervention. She had thought that her meditation was progressing nicely. But Joseph certainly saw how Amanda's fantasies were keeping her from being mindful. Perhaps he also sensed the degree to which she was using her fantasy life to avoid connecting with something more personal, something akin to Winnicott's incommunicado element. By fantasizing much of the time, Amanda was preventing herself from dropping into a less proscribed psychic space. Who knew *what* she might discover if she let go of what she already knew? Joseph's message of "dead end" was consistent with the other teachings of the left-handed path. He was not trying to get Amanda to renounce her desire, only to abandon the compulsive fixations that had hijacked her consciousness. According to the path of desire, renouncing these fixations should open up her longing, not extinguish it.

In Indian thought, the god who most directly embodies this knowledge is Shiva. Shiva, the Lord of Animals and god of destruction, is both a consummate renouncer and an unsurpassable erotic force. He is known for his perpetually erect phallus, his *lingam* of light, which threatens to destroy the world unless it is united with the *yoni*, or vulva, of his lover. But he is also a dweller of the forest, at home in the cremation grounds, the prototype of the wandering ascetic: smeared with ashes, wrapped in snakes and skins, without manners or decorum, a three-eyed drinker of poison known as the Lord of Tears.

Shiva is an ancient god. A four-thousand-year-old image of him survives from the lost Indus Valley civilization showing him sitting in the lotus position surrounded by animals, crowned with the horns of a bull and boasting a huge erection. Many believe that his cult dates back to the sixth millennium B.C. and that his influence can be seen throughout the ancient world, from India to Egypt to Sumer to Crete. Shiva is both a yogi and a lover. When it is called for, his erotic capacity is infinite, as intense as his meditations can be. This makes him a most interesting deity. The Greek Zeus, with his lightning bolt destructive power and unquenchable sexual appetite, was like a sanitized version of him. Shiva embodies the interrelationship of renunciation and desire, of asceticism and eroticism and of destruction and passion that is an inextricable aspect of Indian thought. His complexity is something that the most sophisticated psychoanalyst could appreciate.

Shiva cultivates a substance called *tapas*, the heat of asceticism, something like an alternative Freudian *libido*, that is said to accumulate through the power of yoga and meditation. This heat, derived from the guarding of the senses, inflames the mind of the yogi and gives it resonance. It was this heat that Joseph was encouraging in Amanda. Those who perform austerities, who deliberately withdraw from the pursuit of pleasure, are said to "perform *tapas*." And although it would seem that the accumulation of *tapas* is the precise opposite of the indulgence of desire, in Indian thought this is definitely not the case. "The extreme of one force is the extreme of its opposite; *tapas* and *kama*, interchangeable forms of cosmic heat, replace and limit one another to maintain the balance of the universe."[2] Both desire and *tapas* are forms of heat that can be substituted for one another. They are embers that kindle each other's fire.

This is a very strange concept, and yet it forms the foundation of Indian spirituality. It is played out in the ancient myth of Shiva and reemerges in the Buddhist left-handed path. It can be understood most readily in the famous story of Shiva's destruction of eros. Shiva, it is told, was such a disciplined yogi and had accumulated so much *tapas* that when Kama, the god of passion, disturbed his meditation one day, Shiva reduced him to ashes with a single angry glance from his third eye. It was as if a flash of lightning erupted from his forehead, obliterating the god and his five flowered arrows. But without eros, it is said, the world could not survive. Persuaded of this by his fellow gods, Shiva, with another glance, raised Kama from the dead.

The burning of Kama is one of the acts that Shiva is most

known for, but the resurrection of Kama was an even more astonishing feat. Shiva had the power, accumulated from years of austerities, to burn eros with one look; dispersing desire, it is said, into flowers, mangoes, cuckoos and bees. His meditation was so powerful, his disdain for the world so great, that he could incinerate eros with a mere nod. He was the sine qua non of ascetics. Yet when Shiva asserted his power and reduced Kama to ashes, he saw that the resulting imbalance was not sustainable. As a result, after Kama's resurrection, Shiva emerged from his meditation and embraced his lover Parvati. They commenced a period of sexual intercourse that went on for a thousand years, the bliss of which equaled what he had found in his yoga. Their pleasure, it is said, *was* the divine state, and it was made possible by the heat of their *tapas*. As Shiva and Parvati made abundantly clear, meditation and passion, at least in their case, were two sides of the same coin.

THE SHORES OF THE INFINITE

Shiva's story is relevant to the Dalai Lama's point about renunciation because it indicates, in another way, that the withdrawal in meditation is not done to try to eliminate desire but only to deepen it. By voluntarily forsaking compulsive patterns of thought and behavior, where there are ongoing but futile attempts to get unmet needs satisfied, it is possible to open up other pathways that prove more fulfilling. If people have never felt loved or accepted by their parents, for example, they will be much more likely to find themselves in intimate relationships in which they continue to feel unloved. Then they can try extra hard to make themselves lovable while continuing to feel secretly that there is something wrong with them. Renunciation can be the missing ingredient when patterns like these predominate. It takes the force of will to create circumstances in which something new can happen.

I was reminded of this not too long ago while listening to a visiting Tibetan teacher in the midst of a meditation retreat in rural Connecticut.

"When I first came to this country," the lama recounted, "I thought, 'This is the way children should be raised all over the world.' So careful, so loving, so much attention." In the middle of his dharma talk, he was suddenly speaking quite personally. He had been explaining some of the finer points of what he called "naked awareness," the mind's capacity to see deeply into its own essence. We were on retreat in Litchfield, Connecticut—about seventy of us, practicing together in silence, learning an ancient meditative yoga called "The Great Perfection." But like a tacking sailboat changing direction to stay on a larger course, the lama was now heading down a different path. He screwed up his face mimicking the expression of a doting parent and lapsed into an uncanny imitation. "Here, honey, just try a bite of this. Are you okay with that, sweetie?" Leaning forward, with his shoulders hunched over an imaginary child, he looked for a moment like a mother bird hovering over her nest.

Startled out of my meditative reverie by the lama's impersonation, my attention became very focused. "It's not like in Nepal or Tibet," he continued. "If a child does something wrong, he just gets slapped. Leave him in the corner crying, it doesn't matter. Treated that way, sometimes the child gets a little dull, stops caring about things. That is not so good. But then

I found out, here everyone hates their parents. Relationships are so difficult. In Nepal, this doesn't happen. I can't understand this very well."

As quickly as he brought the subject up, he dropped it again. I found myself wondering if I had even heard him correctly. Usually Tibetan teachers talk only about how *special* mothers are, about how their kindnesses allow us, as totally helpless infants, to survive, over and over again. It is the sort of teaching that we in the West often find refreshing, if slightly intimidating, because we have ignored those basic aspects of the mother-child relationship in favor of more conflicted ones. In an infinite series of multiple lifetimes, the traditional Tibetan argument runs, all beings have in fact been our mothers, and we can cultivate kindness toward them by imagining their prior sacrifices for us. But here was a lama who, however briefly, acknowledged our more difficult relationships with our current parents. He seemed as startled by our difficulties as I had been on first hearing of the meditation wherein all beings are considered mothers. I was intrigued by his candor and disappointed that he did not take the discussion further.

But a day or two later in another talk, the lama, thirty-five-year-old Drubwang Tsoknyi Rinpoche of the Drukpa Kagyu and Nyingpa lineages of Tibetan Buddhism, raised the subject again. In virtually the same language, he expressed astonishment at the level of anger that his Western students seemed to harbor against their parents. Clearly it was bothering him. That night I left a note for the course manager telling him that, unless somebody else volunteered, I could try to explain to the lama why Westerners have such difficult feelings for their parents. The next morning, someone tapped me on the shoulder after a meditation and told me that the lama would meet with me now.

Refreshingly at ease with himself, Tsoknyi Rinpoche was friendly and personable. He brushed aside my efforts at formality and indicated that he was ready to talk right away. We spoke without his interpreter present, so our conversation was restricted to the essentials.

"All that attention comes with a lot of expectations," I began. "Western parents don't feel that their children already are who they are—they feel that it is their job to make them who they should be. They treat their children more as objects than as individuals who already are themselves. Children feel this as a burden."

"A pressure," the lama replied.

"A pressure. And they develop an armor to guard against it. The anger is a reflection of that armor." I thought of a patient of mine as we talked, a young woman who always felt that her parents, in her words, "had a quota on me." She had the feeling that they just couldn't take her, that she was too much for them—too imposing, too difficult, too unrestrained, and at the same time a disappointment: not enough of the right stuff. This woman withdrew from her mother and father, shielding herself from them, but she withdrew from other people in a more generalizable way, and suffered from lack of confidence and isolation as a result. I closed one fist and covered it with my other hand, holding both up to the lama. The closed fist was like the armored child—the hand covering it, the parental expectations.

"All the energy is going into the resistance," I explained. "But inside, the child feels empty. They don't know who they are or what they want. They can't feel their own desire; they know only anger. The anger that comes from being treated as an object. Their emptiness is not like what is described in Buddhism, where emptiness connotes something akin to freedom."

"Hollow," said the lama. He understood.

"In the psychotherapy world, we call that armor 'false self.' A child creates a false self to deal with excessive expectations or with early abandonment: too much parental pressure—or too little. We say there is not enough holding, not just physical holding, but emotional holding, too." I thought to myself about a quotation from Proust, how he explained the caress that allows the infinitude of a person to be felt:

> I might caress her, pass my hand slowly over her, but, just as if I had been handling a stone which encloses the salt of immemorial oceans or the light of a star, I felt that I was touching no more than the sealed envelope of a person who inwardly reached to infinity.[3]

When the false self predominates, there is no sense of that anymore—a person becomes cut off from himself—from his "incommunicado element"—at a deep level.

"The problem with this scenario," I continued, "is that the child often loses touch with who they are on the inside. After a while, they know only the armor, the anger, fear or emptiness. They have a yearning to be known, found or discovered, but no means to make it happen, no trust that it *can* happen. It brings people to places like this." I gestured to indicate the retreat facility.

"Maybe it's not such a bad thing, then!" he smiled.

Tsoknyi Rinpoche was interested in our discussion. "I had

thought of the problem like this," he told me. "Parents seem to see raising their children as only a duty or a job. When the child is grown, they just let go. They are finished. They've done their job, fulfilled their obligations. The child feels cut off—they need that thread."

I thought that he was describing the other side of the same coin. Parents sometimes feel that their only purpose is to help their children separate and individuate, but they think about it in objective terms, as another thing to accomplish. Once it has happened, such parents feel useless or obsolete. Often they divorce as soon as the child leaves for college, throwing the children into crisis just as they are needing to move more deeply into themselves. Compounding the problem is the inevitable estrangement of adolescence, when the first stirrings of grown-up anger make themselves known. Many parents never recover from these upheavals. Their emotional connections with their offspring are so tenuous that when the first expressions of disdain are hurled at them, they retreat forever. Hurt by their children's anger, they feel ignored and unappreciated, not understanding that the child, in addition to wanting to be known by the parents, also wants to know them in a real way.

The lama had discovered for himself a real-life version of what psychotherapists had already figured out. Meditators who came to his retreats to begin a process of gentle introspection came up right away against their childhood pain. While the retreats were designed to teach people how to train their attention to not push away the unpleasant and not cling to the pleasant, what they tended to also do was to put people in a place where they could not avoid how much unfinished business they had. Treated as objects by their well-meaning parents, they were still struggling for subjecthood, but their own tendencies to view their parents as "bad objects" were holding them back from their goals. The lama, I believe, correctly intuited that his students' anger would have to be brought into the field of their meditation. And, like Joseph Goldstein and the Dalai Lama, he also knew that eventually they would have to renounce their efforts to have their parents treat them in a more acceptable manner, that this, too, was a fantasy that could be labeled "dead end." By relinquishing their attachment to achieving this milestone, they could learn how not to make the same mistake. They could stop treating their parents as bad objects, and begin to explore themselves as subjects: breaking down the false self that obscured the light within.

In Kahlil Gibran's famous work *The Prophet*, a beautiful description of this same double-edged truth is found:

> *Your joy is your sorrow unmasked*
> *The selfsame well from which your laughter rises was often-times filled with your tears.*
> *And how else can it be?*
> *The deeper that sorrow carves into your being, the more joy you can contain.*[4]

This final image, of sorrow carving into the soul, is an apt description of the dynamic that exists between renunciation and desire. Just as sorrow, in Gibran's vision, creates a space that joy can fill, so does renunciation create a space that desire can more freely inhabit. By turning away from the compulsive dead ends of clinging, possession and consumption, a person can learn to dwell more fully in themselves. The hotter the flame of a meditator's *tapas,* the stronger the spirit of emergence. The more a person has seen his own clinging, the less the need to get in the way of intimate connection. As Shiva found when he turned toward Parvati, the bliss of yoga and the bliss of desire are interchangeable. Both wash us up on the shores of the infinite.

· III ·

THE END
OF CLINGING

"Like a coward, like a common ordinary stage-actor you traded her over to another. You told her to go to him though you'd long loved her. Why do you serve Ravana as best you may, and give him Sita for his pleasure? You forsake her. She is encircled by evil . . . do not be a meek little man . . . I said never fear to love well," said Hanuman. "If you can't bear it who will?"

Ramayana *(p. 270)*

7

From Object to Subject

In an uncanny parallel between the world of psychotherapy and the world of Indian spirituality, the metamorphosis of desire that both disciplines envision is equated with an opening to the feminine. The more commonly accepted form of desire, the one that is usually associated with masculine energy, is the familiar one of possession, acquisition and objectification. In this version of desire, the self actively tries to get its needs met by manipulating its environment, extracting what it requires from a world that is consistently objectified. But it is this version of desire that tends toward frustration and disappointment, that can never be entirely satisfied. The paradox of desire is that we are actually seeking another mode altogether, one that we have trouble imagining, or acknowledging. This is where both the psychoanalytic and the Indian spiritual worlds are helpful.

By articulating this alternative mode as a feminine one, they show us what we are missing in ourselves. As D.W. Winnicott succinctly put it, "The male element *does* while the female element (in males and females) *is*."[1] The male element is involved in activity, while the female element is all about being. While desire's masculine energies are necessary, they are not, by themselves, sufficient. Desire, in its longing for completion, is ultimately in search of being.

In the *Ramayana*, it is the female protagonist, Sita, who must discover and stay true to her own voice while her lover battles to reclaim her. All of Rama's male energy goes into this effort. Both Sita and Rama must come into a new relationship with Sita's deepening desire, with her newly won female capacity. This is the direct outcome of the first three steps of the left-handed path: entering the gap between satisfaction and fulfillment, honestly confronting the manifestations of clinging and renouncing the compulsive thoughts and behaviors that clinging provokes. Working with desire in this way allows for a growing appreciation of the feminine. Nor is this insight limited to the *Ramayana*. In the Indian myth of Shiva, his yogic renunciation not only brings him into harmony with his lover Parvati but also, in a further development that only the most outrageous psychoanalyst could imagine, reveals his own hermaphroditic nature. In the most esoteric portraits of Shiva, it turns out, he is found to possess both phallus and vulva. While he represents, in most instances, a classic male position, complete with erect phallus and unsurpassable energy, he is also revealed to be thoroughly at home with his female side, as exemplified not only by his female sexual organs, but also by the Ganges River, symbol of the mother, flowing from his hair. And even in the relatively staid world of Buddhism, the loosening of desire's fixed agenda—its relaxation—strikes a note that is eerily resonant with recent breakthroughs in psychoanalytic theory, in which the perspective of female analysts has finally been given its due. The Buddha, it must be pointed out, assumes an androgynous figure throughout much of Asian art.

THE BIRTH OF THE SUBJECT

In her now classic book on woman's desire, the psychoanalyst Jessica Benjamin described this missing element very well. She recounted a poignant vignette. Two psychologists, one of them the mother of an infant boy, were strolling by the hospital nursery one day when they stopped to peer through a glass partition at the other newborns. On each bassinet were pink or blue labels announcing the sex of the child for all to see. The blue labels for the boys jauntily proclaimed, "I'm a boy!" but, to their astonishment, the pink labels for the girls did not correspond. Instead of "I'm a girl!" the pink ones all read, "It's a girl!" All the boys were "I" and all the girls were "It." The boys were given a subjective voice, the voice of desire, but the girls were offered to the world as objects. The sight of the baby girls, already bound by society's preconceptions, was an epiphany for Benjamin. Freud's perennial question, "What does woman want?" was not phrased correctly, she concluded. The question is not *what* do they want, but *do* they want, at all. Do they *have* their own desire? Or perhaps the question might be more correctly stated: Can women *be* their desire? The challenge for women, she decided, is to move from being just an object of desire to becoming a subject: *she who desires*.[2]

In formulating things this way, Benjamin made a major contribution to the understanding of what makes passion passionate.

She charted a course that we can also see described in the ancient *Ramayana* epic, in which Sita found herself stolen away from an undifferentiated union with Rama and became the object of Ravana's lust. Refusing to capitulate to this objectified status, Sita deepened her own desire while held captive on the island of Lanka, making possible an eventual reunion with her lover once he reached her in her newly discovered subjectivity. Sita made the journey from object to subject that Benjamin described, and then demanded that Rama come to her, even though the magical Hanuman was completely capable of spiriting her off the island and back to her lover. In making this demand of Rama, Sita insisted that he find and recognize her current inner life, so that the two dimensions of desire could become one. She gave new purpose to his male element. In so doing, she made possible a fresh experience for both of them, that which can only unfold between two subjects. This is the journey that desire wants to take us on: one that cuts through the limitations of both subject and object and opens up the playful possibilities of mutuality, passion and affection that are dependent on the capacity to be.

Benjamin's contribution to the psychology of desire was crucial because she was able to differentiate its two distinct aspects: one that she initially equated with the male and one with the female. The male desire, as male psychoanalysts have conceived of it for a long time, is represented by the phallus. It knows what it wants. In a child's psyche (according to the psychoanalytic tradition), the phallus, emblem of the father, stands for separation from the mother and for an independent life in the world. Because the father is perceived by the child to have a self-sufficient life outside of the household, his sexual organ takes on the connotations of this autonomy. It becomes the antidote to the all-powerful maternal presence, the fundamental expression of an alternative. As a representation of an active agency apart from the maternal environment, the phallus comes to represent the seeking of satisfaction outside the protection of the mother. For a girl it might take the form of fantasies of having her own baby or discovering her own body rather than having a penis, but the psychic function is the same: The need is for an alternative to, and an escape from, the demands of the home environment.

For young boys, according to this theory, the process of identification with the father makes assuming their own desire relatively straightforward; but for young girls, especially those with controlling mothers, the process is more complex. Differentiation is more problematic. The phallus might still be the most prominent psychic symbol of separation and individuation, but it is more difficult for a young girl to identify with it than it is for a boy. This is where the concept of penis envy comes in. "Penis envy is not an end in itself," wrote one of the first feminist psychoanalysts to untangle the sexual symbolism of the psyche, "but rather the expression of a desire to triumph over the omnipotent primal mother through the possession of the organ the mother lacks, i.e., the penis. Penis envy seems to be as proportionately intense as the maternal imag[e] is powerful."[3] For a girl in such situations, the phallus is the symbol of the way out of the relationship with the mother. The French feminists, with their characteristic bravado, say that the phallus "beats back the mother" in a young girl's imagination. Possessing, or being possessed by, a man, especially a self-inflated one, functions as a bulwark against the seemingly overwhelming nature of the mother-daughter relationship. A classic example of this might be the decision of an overprotected and obedient daughter to date a young man with a motorcycle while away at college. The "phallic" symbolism of the motorcycle—dangerous, powerful and alluring—helps such a young woman put distance between herself and her mother.

AN OUNCE OF SPACE

In Benjamin's view, the phallus serves a similar symbolic function in both young boys and young girls: it is cherished as a means of individuation and as an expression of active desire.[4] But there is another dimension to desire that she gendered as feminine, although it is clearly an aspect that is shared by both sexes. This feminine desire is not for penetration but for space. The space that is longed for is not just a space within, as a concrete equation with the vagina might lead one to suspect, but is for a space that is also without: a space *between* individuals that makes room for the individuality of both parties and for meetings at the edge. It is a space that permits discovery of one's own voice. It is this that Sita found in her isolation and imprisonment in Lanka.

Perhaps a vignette from one of my patients can help explain what this means. Andrea was a young doctor in training: smart, beautiful, independent and just engaged to be married. Her fiancé was older, a writer who worked mostly at home. They had recently moved in together in a small apartment in Queens. Andrea's fiancé was clearly in love with her, but he sometimes seemed excessively needy of her presence. He would drop everything when she walked in the door and hover around her. She longed for a return to the early days of their courtship, when he had seemed more remote and she had been able to pursue and even seduce him. Now he was so available. Andrea recounted a small event from a recent evening together when he had eagerly pulled her toward him as she was getting into bed, both of them knowing they were about to have sex. He was already under the sheets and she was just climbing onto the bed when he reached for her.

"Just give me an ounce of space to love you from," Andrea had said at the time, but he had felt rejected by her spontaneous comment and threatened to go sleep on the couch. She had just wanted to get under the sheets before he grabbed her, she told me, wondering why he had objected so vehemently to her comment.

Andrea wanted to be more in contact with her own desire. Her fiancé's need for her made it too difficult for her to stay in touch with herself; his desire tended to take over and she lost the sense of separateness that allowed her to know her own longing. She could experience his "male" desire, but it made her feel as if she were just an energy source that he needed to tap, rather than a person in her own right. Since he was so offended by her attempts to confront him, we worked to develop her capacity to stay in touch with herself, even while permitting him to feel close to her. Andrea felt obligated by her boyfriend's affection, and she felt that she had only two choices: to submit, and lose herself, or push him away. Rather than seeing things this way, I tried to help her feel less swayed by his need, allowing him to calm down so that she could see something more than his dependence on her. While she might not be able to pursue and seduce him as she once had, from this place of calm she could still reach out for him, an agent in her own right.

Benjamin's vision of feminine desire describes an interpersonal expanse within which lies the potential for both self-discovery and connection. She echoes the findings of the seventeenth-century Indian mystics who determined that the flavor of separation was the most critical ingredient in an erotic relationship. This is a concept that can be found all over the world. In Japanese garden design, there is an important organizing principle called *miegakure*, or "hide-and-reveal," that portrays this truth in another way. In a Japanese garden, only a part of any object is ever made visible—the whole is never exposed. It is commonplace, for example, to have a meandering waterfall come in and out of the line of vision of someone walking a path. Each new view allows the waterfall to be temporarily glimpsed from a different perspective, imparting "not only an illusion of depth but also the impression that there are hidden beauties beyond."[5] The eye is teased by the water—we see it, then lose it, then find it again as we wind our way through the garden. By preventing the object from ever being known completely, the design encourages the viewer to imagine the invisible parts. The result is just what my patient Andrea was longing for in her relationship: "a sense of vastness in a small space,"[6] the feeling of mystery that keeps something interesting even when it is known very well.

It was this vastness that Andrea missed with her fiancé, confined as she was in the limited space of her new relationship. She needed more hiddenness in order to open up the possibilities of play that move a sexual relationship into the realm of eros.[7] When there is room for two subjects, a relationship becomes more like a Japanese garden. A call and response of sounds, gestures, feelings and sensations can unfold that allow unfurling desires to be known, appreciated, delighted in, and returned. The result allows something akin to what the British psychoanalyst Masud Khan once called an "ego-orgasm,"[8] the intimacy that comes when emotional surrender joins with physical release. When Andrea felt that she was nothing more than an energy source for her boyfriend, this kind of mutuality did not seem possible between them. While he might have been the "I" in the relationship, he was still relating to her too exclusively as an "it."

BEING VERSUS DOING

The tribulations of another recent patient of mine, Tina, help to flesh some of this out. Tina was a talented teacher in a local private high school, kindhearted, smart and amiable. Catholic, the daughter of a wealthy New Jersey family, she was all too conscious of her beauty, or, it might be more accurate to say, of the fragility of her beauty. It was the primary link between her and her mother. Discussions of food, of what was fattening, of how much each of them ate, and of how their weight fluctuated dominated their interactions. But the price of this closeness was a secretiveness that Tina developed around food and a heightened concern about her body image.

Tina was in her early thirties when she came to see me and had had a succession of boyfriends since her late teens. One of the issues she brought up in her first session with me was her discomfort when her current boyfriend attempted to have oral sex with her. Always conscious of how her body looked, Tina was disturbed at the idea of a man "going down" on her. All she could think about was how "gross" it must be. Only when she had some alcohol to drink could Tina begin to explore cunnilingus, but she found on several occasions that, although her boyfriend assured her that she had enjoyed (and even initiated) the activity, she had no memory of it. She was obviously worried about where she was heading.

Tina was stuck in an object-based mode of relating. She could only think of herself through the eyes of another: be it her mother checking to see how fat she was, or her boyfriend (in her imagination) evaluating the attractiveness of her body. Her fears of oral sex were probably indications of this object-based mode, as she seemed to experience her boyfriends primarily as "devouring objects" intent on making food out of her. The space of her own subjectivity, her own emotional experience, was not safe or available in such circumstances—it seemed to open only when she shared her inner experiences with her closest girlfriend. Luckily for Tina, soon after she started therapy she met a man whom she felt an immediate kinship with. While he was less sexually experienced than many of her previous boyfriends, she found, to her surprise, that she was not inhibited in speaking her mind to him. Although he could certainly be self-involved at times, he always respected her insights. They shared a sense of humor and formed a close friendship while beginning a sexual relationship. Soon they moved in together and relocated to another city. Tina left therapy with me. Her belated movement from object to subject had begun.

While the psychoanalytic formula spelled out by Benjamin affords the male the first subjective sense of agency, it is a mistake to think that the need to shift from an object-based mode is solely the journey of the woman. Whether a man is seeking an object or a woman makes herself into one, the mode of relating is the same. Both parties have the potential to see things differently. Desire, while it can be inflamed under the object mode, is unlikely to be satisfied with it. It is much more likely to be diverted into clinging in the frantic effort to secure some kind of unforthcoming security. The opening up of subjective appreciation, on the other hand, involves a recognition of the unpossessability of the other. This recognition, which literally "gives space," allows desire to operate as it would in a well-crafted Japanese garden. Since the other is never capable of being totally revealed, he or she is also capable of being continually inspiring. Desire feeds off otherness, and otherness inspires desire.

The journey from an object-based way of relating to one that permits two subjects is begun in early childhood, but it is rarely completed then. If we are lucky, it can be continued in intimate sexual relations and further elaborated in meditation and spiritual life, or developed in meditation and brought to fruition in sexual intimacy. This progression is one of the links among emotional, relational, and spiritual life that coalesces in the path of desire. It can be talked about in mythic, psychodynamic, sexual or sacred terms, but at its core is the need for the "male"-based objective mode to be balanced by the "female"-based subjective one. This is no easy task. To give up the conviction that people can be related to as objects (or "energy sources") is harder than it sounds. If people are not objects, then how can we think about them? Our minds balk, the way they do when trying to understand Einsteinian relativity or the wavelike nature of a photon. We are conditioned to think in terms of things, not in terms of unknown processes like ungraspable personal subjectivities. Our language even stumbles over them. Yet our own desire keeps revealing the insufficiency of the object model.

While the primary function of formal Buddhist meditation is to create the possibility of the experience of "being," my work as a therapist has shown me that the demands of intimate life can be just as useful as meditation in moving people toward this capacity. Just as in formal meditation, intimate relationships teach us that the more we relate to each other as objects, the greater our disappointment. The trick, as in meditation, is to use this disappointment to change the way we relate. Out of our failure to find a compliant object can come the appreciation of others as subjects in their own right. While we might sometimes feel frustrated by their failures to give us what we think we need, this very frustration has within it the spirit of emergence. For when we accept the fact that no adult person can satisfy all of our needs, we are on the road to appreciating our adult partners for who they are, not for who we wish they would be. It is this scenario that Benjamin's understanding of "male" and "female" sought to explain. The "female" desire for space is an expression of a need that both sexes have. It is a need that Winnicott expressed most succinctly in his famous phrase, "It is joy to be hidden, but disaster not to be found,"[9] a need for recognition of one's self as a subject.

But a subject is not an object. While it can be found, it cannot be captured. Finding it is more of an ongoing process of discovery than it is a onetime act. The acceptance of an inner, private, personal and even silent aspect of self and other is a gift that opens up a continuing exchange with the world. This is the secret capacity that desire is in search of, a capacity for "being" that can only be found when the more dominant need to "do" is undone. In this light, it is no longer so mysterious what a woman wants. Like a man, she wants a partner who cares what she wants, someone who desires her desire, and is able to dwell in the space it creates.

8

A Facilitating Environment

In 1912, Henri Matisse visited Morocco and was struck by the softness of the light there. It changed the way he approached painting. Trying to express the spirituality that he felt in that light, he began to remove many of the features that he would ordinarily have included on his canvas. Faces became impersonal, stripped of the attributes that give them their individuality. Outlines of objects vanished and uninterrupted areas of pure color began to emerge. No Western painter had ever taken such liberties. It was a technique that came to be known as "less is more," and it allowed Matisse the freedom, warmth and exuberance that was to define his work.[1] In letting go of the conventional approach to representation, a spirit of emergence took hold. In a manner completely consistent with Benjamin's description of the discovery of the "feminine," Matisse opened himself to another way of experiencing the world. Painting has not been the same since.

Something similar happened to my friend Jack Engler when he first came to India in 1975, although it was not painting that changed as a result, it was his understanding of desire. Jack is a psychotherapist as well as a Buddhist teacher, and in that year he was just beginning his exploration of Buddhist philosophy after completing strenuous training in clinical psychology. After his very first meditation retreat with Joseph Goldstein, Jack Kornfield and Sharon Salzberg in Bucksport, Maine, Jack left for India for what would be a two-year immersion in Buddhist studies. As a Western psychologist just awakening to the power of Buddhist psychology, Jack was, to say the least, enthusiastic in his pursuit of Buddhist wisdom. While he had begun to confront his own clinging, his mind was still driven by the forces of habit and conditioning that we all must struggle with if we are to engage with this path. Suffice it to say that Jack arrived in India with a Western mind-set toward Buddhism. Like Ravana spying Sita for the first time, he wanted to make it his, as quickly as possible.

LESS IS MORE

Jack traveled to Bodh Gaya, a tiny village in the north of India that is the site of the historical Buddha's enlightenment. A descendant of the original *bodhi* tree, under which the Buddha sat when he achieved his awakening, still thrives in the village, and, while the town is small and dusty, with not much more than a couple of streets and several tea stalls set up to feed the steady trickle of Western pilgrims, each Buddhist country in Asia maintains a small temple devoted to the study of Buddhism. A large *stupa*, dating from medieval times, rises behind the *bodhi* tree, giving a hint of what must have been a sacred center of Buddhism in the previous millennium.

Jack came to Bodh Gaya to study with a remarkable Bengali man named Anagarika Munindra, who had been a teacher to Joseph Goldstein over the previous seven or eight years. Munindra was born in Bangladesh, a descendant of Buddhists who had been forced east by social upheavals in the eleventh century. He worked in the 1940s for the Mahabodhi Society of India, an organization dedicated to preserving what was left of Buddhism in India, and in the 1950s became superintendent of the temple in Bodh Gaya. But Munindra realized that while he knew Buddhist history, he did not really understand Buddhist practice, which had fallen into decline in his own country. In the 1950s, therefore, he traveled to Burma to study under a meditation master named Mahasi Sayadaw, who was one of the teachers most responsible for rediscovering and promulgating Buddhist mindfulness practice in the twentieth century. Munindra studied with Sayadaw off and on for nine years, mastering the teachings of Buddhist psychology and reaching the various levels of insight associated with an understanding of "no-self." Through his teaching of Joseph Goldstein, Jack Engler, and scores of other Westerners who traveled to Bodh Gaya to learn from him, he became a critical figure in the transmission of Buddhism to the West.

Munindra was an iconoclastic individual, not exactly the picture of an enlightened teacher that one might imagine. I met him myself on a number of occasions and was always a bit taken aback. Just as Shiva in the Indian myths could embody someone both completely of the world and simultaneously apart from it, Munindra seemed to be constantly undercutting the image of how an awakened person should behave. This is part of what made him such an exemplary teacher. For one thing, he talked all the time. He was a chatterbox. For another, he seemed completely comfortable in the world, not removed from it. Joseph Goldstein's memories reinforce the colorful aspects of his teacher's character. He tells of a time when he spied Munindra in the bazaar, bargaining vigorously with the local vendors over the price of some peanuts. Munindra looked a lot like Ben Kingsley in his role as Mahatma Gandhi; he was a small, wiry man, dressed always in white robes, with dark eyeglasses and an excitable temperament. I imagine the local villagers found him somewhat intimidating. Joseph felt embarrassed to see his venerable teacher haggling with the native merchants. The price he was arguing about, after all, probably amounted to less than a nickel.

"Munindraji," Joseph finally asked him, "Why are you getting so caught up in bargaining for a handful of peanuts? We thought you told us to be simple and easy."

Munindra was amused at Joseph's concern.

"You need to be simple—not a simpleton," he replied.

When Jack Engler arrived in Bodh Gaya in 1975, Munindra was there to greet him. Jack had flown straight to Calcutta, spent several days there and then took an all-night train to Gaya, the nearest railway station. Not knowing that it was possible to get to Bodh Gaya from Gaya by bus, he then took an even more exhausting rickshaw ride—four or five hours in length—from the railway station to the Tourist Bungalow in Bodh Gaya. He arrived cold, tired, hungry, embarrassed at having paid too much to his rickshaw driver, and pretty disoriented. But with an eagerness that I have come to associate with naive desire, whether it be in the East or the West, the first thing he said to Munindra was, "I'm here! I'm ready! When do I begin?"

Munindra's reply took Jack off guard.

"How are your bowel movements?" he asked.

As a matter of fact, they were not very good. Actually, they were pretty bad. Munindra, whose father had been an ayurvedic physician, spent the next two weeks teaching Jack about the power of garlic pills to clean him out and fleaseed husk to stop him up. They did not talk of much else. As Jack now says, "He had his priorities straight, even if I didn't."[2]

Munindra's dexterity in dealing with Jack's desire was instructive. While he never addressed it head on, he was careful, in all the time that Jack spent under his tutelage, to always expand or broaden what Jack was after, rather than gratifying him directly. In the two years that Jack studied Buddhism with him, Munindra asked him about his meditation only twice. He never gave him explicit instruction about practice. This is from a man who was one of the foremost meditation instructors of the twentieth century, revered for his own meditative accomplishments. Yet he was very careful not to overtly respond to, or reject, Jack's demands. Instead, like the Moroccan light that softened Matisse's palette, Munindra gentled Jack's desire. He nourished it, but not by satisfying it too readily. In the Dalai Lama's vernacular, he was creating the circumstances in which a spirit of emergence could be born, in which Jack could renounce his preconceived notions about Buddhism in order to discover it for himself. From a psychodynamic point of view, we might say that Munindra was showing Jack that meditation was not something that he had to *do*, but could only be something that he *was*. Without explicitly gendering it, Munindra was nevertheless opening up the feminine side of things.

One afternoon, when Jack was interviewing Munindra for his doctoral research, Munindra suggested that they take a walk together behind the Chinese temple where he was then living. While taking their break, Jack asked him suddenly, "Munindraji, what is the dharma?" Perhaps Jack was frustrated at Munindra's elusive style of teaching or at his own progress, or lack thereof, since arriving in India. Or perhaps he was sincerely trying to dig deeper into the Buddha's teachings. In trying to pinpoint the dharma, he was asking about the core teaching of the Buddha, his "truth" or his "way," the traditional, and imperfect, translations of the word. It was a very important question and, to my mind, Jack's asking it echoed the intensity of his desire upon first arriving in Bodh Gaya. There was a certain impatience in his approach.

Munindra's reply surprised Jack.

"Dharma is living the life fully," he replied.

At the time, Jack was struck by the response. It sounded like one of those comments that bore further contemplation. It certainly challenged the conventional view of dharma as a turning away from life. He made a mental note to think about it later but basically let it go in one ear and out the other. Yet as the years went by, this comment of Munindra's gradually became Jack's own personal koan, one that he continues to ponder. And it came to embody Munindra's teachings for him, just as the softness of the Moroccan light continued to suffuse the paintings of Matisse, long after he returned to his native country.

STILLNESS AND URGENCY

Munindra's comment can be read in a number of ways. In suggesting that dharma means living life fully, he was impressing upon Jack that no aspect of his personal experience needed to be rejected. With such an inclusive vision, even desire could be treated in the "simple and easy" manner that Munindra encouraged. In suggesting that he live life fully, Munindra was inspiring Jack to relax his desire, to be simple and easy with it, too.

He was also obliquely recasting the teachings of the Buddhist stupas, in which the joys and pleasures of the everyday world beckon the pilgrim toward the center, where the heart of the Buddhist teachings on emptiness and impermanence reside. By opening to the desires of the everyday world, these monuments suggest, we can continue to open to the desires of the spiritual world. They are not in opposition to each other, but are different aspects of the same mandala, with one serving as a portal into the other, as the arches decorated with erotic scenes open into the meditation spaces that circle the central void. In true Buddhist fashion, Munindra was undermining the most common psychological stance that we bring to our lives: the belief in ourselves as isolated, alone and in need, the attachment to the separate self. When we approach the world in this way, what we get from it is never enough. The object always disappoints, leaving us clinging to it or feeling rejected, thrown back into our isolated and insecure position. This is the approach that Jack was unconsciously embodying and the one that Munindra was refusing to be engaged by. He did not want to let Jack's desire become a problem, reinforcing his sense of isolation instead of ushering him toward spiritual understanding.

Finally, in Munindra's deft handling of Jack's eager question-ing, we can glimpse the workings of a contemporary Buddhist master. While Jack was a therapist who came to India seeking spirituality, what he found was something of equal relevance to the world of psychotherapy. In his interactions, Munindra chal-lenged Jack's unconscious clinging, not by attacking it directly, but by catching Jack off guard, surprising him, and refusing to meet his expectations. He consistently deflected Jack's desire, revealing to him that there was another way of approaching what he was after. When Jack came looking for the dharma, first Munindra pointed him back to his neglected physical self and then insisted that he widen his view to make the dharma the whole world. He loosened Jack up and modeled an alterna-tive psychological stance. We can be different, he seemed to suggest, less defended, more relaxed, more porous and open, simpler, easier, and still ourselves. And the route to this change is not by cutting off desire, but by expanding our usual under-standing of it. In his own way, Munindra was articulating the age-old wisdom embodied in the myth of Shiva as well as the psychoanalytic understanding of the importance of the femi-nine. Renunciation of a hurried, hungry desire deepens the ca-pacity for a more passionate engagement with the world.

Munindra's role in shaking up Jack's orientation to the world was critical. In this way, he was the quintessential spiri-tual teacher. Jack thought he knew what he was doing in India (studying the dharma), but Munindra wanted him to live it, not just put it under a microscope. In encouraging Jack to grow into himself, he demonstrated an important principle of Buddhism. Jack thought he knew who he was, what he was after and how he was going to find it, but Munindra could see where he was stuck. His job as a teacher was to make his student aware, free-ing him so that his desire could take him where he needed to go, not where he thought he was headed. In order to accomplish this, Munindra gave Jack the space that Jack needed to develop in himself.

INTERMEDIATE AREA

The mental state that Munindra encouraged in his students has an important parallel in psychotherapy. In modeling and encouraging a state in which he was "simple and easy," open, undefended and without preconceived notions or expectations, Munindra was creating what, in psychoanalysis, is called a facilitating environment. A facilitating environment is one that a parent creates for a child in which the child's defenses can be let down, when a child can "simply be" without worrying about keeping things together. In a facilitating environment, a child is free to explore his or her own inner world, to try to come to terms with the paradoxical nature of separation from and connection to the parents. The facilitating environment promotes growth because it gives the child room to move away from the parents while staying present enough not to provoke anxiety. It allows a child what Winnicott called "transitional experiencing."[3]

The key to understanding transitional experiencing is child's play. When a relatively secure child plays with his or her toys, the entire room comes alive. It is not a question of a "self" playing with "objects," but of an animation of the entire space. Winnicott called this the "intermediate area" of experience, and spoke of the fluidity or flow that comes when a child is able to relax ego boundaries and invest playthings with his or her imagination, with his or her self. This capacity, he proposed, is at the root of creative expression.

One of the important fruits of the path of desire is that this "intermediate area" becomes accessible once again. When desire is opened up so that it is no longer exclusively attacking the object in a hurried and hungry manner but can patiently give the object space, a deeper intimacy and a more secure attachment become possible. Munindra's interactions with Jack gave him just this kind of experience: he wanted Jack to live his life fully, not partially, to slow down so that his own agenda did not obscure greater possibilities. But one does not have to travel to India, or Morocco, to reap the benefits of this shift. Sometimes it is possible in one's very own home.

One of my patients, Flora, a forty-five-year-old mother of two, told me a story recently about an interaction she had with her ten-year-old daughter that describes a different version of this same scenario. Flora's daughter had bunk beds in her room, left over from when she was younger. One day, while her daughter was in school, Flora moved the upper bunk into her other child's room. She did not just spring this change on her daughter—they had talked about it before—but it was still a shock. Her daughter went into a rage when she came home, and Flora was at a loss about how to handle it. She was a firm mother, and her impulse was to come down hard. Her desire was certainly for an end to the problem as soon as possible. But Flora had been learning to meditate, and the first lesson of her meditation was to observe her own reactions, rather than acting on them precipitously. Somehow, she thought of this as her daughter was becoming enraged. Rather than telling her to grow up, she just waited. She did nothing, but stayed attentive as her daughter cried and screamed. Soon, her daughter began to talk. It seems that the mattress had magical powers. If it were tampered with, her daughter would have bad luck. There was a similar property to her socks, which helped explain why she insisted on wearing the same pair each day. Flora's mother, who had been a very important part of the household, had recently died, a loss that the whole family was just starting to deal with, and this kind of magical thinking was one of Flora's daughter's ways of handling her anxiety. Once it was expressed to her mother, the objects were no longer so important to her. Her mother's willingness not to react had opened up a space that could hold the anxiety by itself. A deeper intimacy between mother and daughter grew out of Flora's ability to restrain her initial impulses.

In Winnicott's view, much of our suffering stems from a lost capacity for this sort of waiting, an exclusive reliance on the male, object-seeking, mode of relating. Without it, we are stuck in our reactions, never an entirely satisfactory place to be. As he described it, "The person we are trying to help needs a new experience in a specialized setting. The experience is one of a non-purposive state, as one might say a sort of ticking over of the unintegrated personality."[4] Winnicott's words are instructive, and the parallels to Munindra's approach are not accidental. Desire cannot always be satisfied by attacking the problem, or by trying to possess or control the object. Sometimes an entirely different mode is required, one in which the self is relinquished instead of indulged, where completion is found through subtraction rather than addition.

In his descriptions of "a non-purposive state," Winnicott was unknowingly going to the heart of Buddhism. This is what Munindra showed to Jack: that it is possible to stay open and desirous without jumping at the first, and most obvious, possibility. Non-purposive means having no fixed agenda, but it does not mean being closed or shut down. It is the approach that gives access to the "female" dimension of space, the one that facilitates growth. And an unintegrated personality is one in which all the effort is not going into maintaining a false front. Meditation, like Winnicott's psychotherapy, is a way of creating this environment for the self. As Flora found, it can also create it for another.

When my son was eleven, he had a dog that he slept with every night, not a real dog but a stuffed animal who had kept him company since he was young. He came into my son's life when we were on a trip to Tucson many years ago, so he tended to speak (when I made him talk) with something of a Western twang. He reminded me, for some reason I have not bothered to analyze, of Michael Landon's hefty brother in the old television show *Bonanza*, so, even though my children have never seen that show, we called him Hoss. Hoss is what is traditionally known as a *transitional object*—he serves as a bridge between child and parent, a source of comfort with a peculiar status somewhere between self and other, a portal to the intermediate area that Winnicott described so well. In our household, this transitional object had also assumed the power of speech, so he tended to function, at times when I was present, as some kind of alter ego for me.

I did not generally plan ahead of time what Hoss would say, so all kinds of strange things tended to come out of his mouth. He had taken to calling my son "Little Pardner," for example, and to delivering such homilies as, "Don't drink and drive," and "The Wheel of Fortune is always turning, sometimes you're up, and sometimes you're down." I figured it was better for Hoss to say those kinds of things than for me to always be repeating them, so he tended to say them a lot. When pressed, Hoss traced his origins to Boone County in the state of Kentucky (where my wife's brother and his wife and children live), and he has provided a sketchy childhood history of sleeping in a shed in the backyard of his parents' home. He does not talk that much anymore, perhaps a sentence or two at night before the lights get turned off, but in earlier years he was known to engage in whole conversations. In the days after the World Trade Center tragedy, however, Hoss found himself in a whole new kind of exchange.

We live in lower Manhattan, just outside of the area that was most severely disrupted by the collapse of the towers. We had a view of them from our front windows before the disaster, and my son could see them on fire from his science classroom at school in Brooklyn Heights on the morning of September 11th. For weeks after their collapse we had to pass through police or army checkpoints to reach our house and for months, depending on the direction of the wind, the air we breathed was fouled with acrid-smelling smoke. There was rarely a day not filled with graphic reminders of the destruction. It was as if a big gash had been riven through our neighborhood, and an equally big one through our psyches. My wife and I, like grown-ups everywhere, were in a state of almost unceasing worry and agitation.

Into this maelstrom strode Hoss. A couple of nights after the terrorist attack, my son suddenly initiated a conversation with him. We were back in our house, after having spent one night at a friend's in Brooklyn. The swirl of sirens surrounded us as we went about our evening rituals.

"Hey Hoss," my son called out. "Did you hear what happened to the World Trade Center?"

We were alone in his bedroom, getting ready to read stories before going to sleep. I suddenly felt more alert.

"Can't say that I have, Little Pardner," Hoss replied. My heart was beating fast, and I knew I had to buy some time. It was not like the kids had been communicating much of what was in their minds about the catastrophe. "What happened to the World Trade Center?" Hoss asked innocently.

Hoss was probably the only person in the world not to know what had happened, but that seemed not to bother my son. It left him in a position to impart some essential information.

"The terrorists hijacked two airplanes and flew them into the World Trade Center and they collapsed. You didn't hear about that, Hoss?"

One of the things that was interesting about this discussion was observing my son when he was in the midst of it. He was so focused. Play, as the Swiss developmental psychologist Jean Piaget often said, is a child's work. Hoss was lying on the bed, I was in a chair on the other side of the room, and my son was jumping around between us. It was not as if he thought he was talking directly to the animal—it was very clear to all of us that I was the one doing the responding. Yet there was a willing suspension of disbelief that allowed the conversation to unfold. He knew that it was me he was talking to, but he knew just as well that it was not me. There was a cheerfulness to his interaction that was not present in the rest of his encounters with grownups during this overwhelmingly glum moment in our lives together. He was clearly delighted to be able to tell Hoss the bad news. And I had one of those split-second decisions to make. How was Hoss going to respond? Were I to listen to my own agenda, I would have tried to be reassuring at that moment, or perhaps "therapeutic," quizzing my son about how he had been feeling over the past few days. But luckily, I sensed an alternative. I was willing to suspend my own disbelief also. The words poured out of my mouth.

"What are you talking about, Little Pardner? Terrorists, hijackings, buildings collapsing! Listen to you. What kind of imagination do you have? People don't fly airplanes into skyscrapers, you know that!"

We started to laugh, the first laughter since the horrible events began to churn. Hoss was clearly speaking the truth, the truth as we used to know it. And I was getting to say, in play, what I could no longer say in fact. On the small stage of a child's bedroom, the old truth and the new truth were sorting themselves out.

My wife and daughter heard us laughing and came running in.

"Hoss doesn't believe me about the hijackers," my son gasped. "He thinks I'm making it up."

I think we were experiencing what the national television audience experienced when David Letterman did his first post-apocalyptic late-night talk show. The courage and the relief of laughter. Things seemed suddenly much more in balance. Although he was completely wrong, Hoss was absolutely right. People don't fly airplanes into skyscrapers. But the only one who could now affirm such a thing was a stuffed animal who could not even really talk. Relief streamed down my son's face as he told Hoss the story of the past several days.

I felt very lucky to have stumbled into this exchange at such a critical time. Something essential happened that allowed for the processing of the terrible information at an emotional level.

We all knew the facts by this time, but we had not really begun digesting our feelings. We needed each other to do that, and it helped to have an inanimate, yet animated, object to serve as an intermediary between us. It was as if we could pour our feelings back and forth through Hoss, as if he were a vessel that held our emotions as they passed through him. He was our Hanuman, the bridge between self and other that allowed two subjective realities, two people, to move in and out of each other.

I have a friend who told me that she left her television on night and day for seventy-two hours after September 11th, even when she slept or left the house, out of fear that she might miss something, and out of the need for comfort and closeness. This is the state that many of us were in for months after the onset of the terrorist threat. But the ready access to so much information put many people in a compromised position. We are the only animal that in the face of trauma continues to re-traumatize itself, playing and replaying that which has already happened to frighten us. In fact, while our language tells us that what we are doing is playing and replaying, in truth we do exactly the opposite. We do not play, as my son was doing with Hoss; we repeat. Endlessly rewinding the trauma, we etch it ever more concretely into our psyches, even as we desire the very comfort and closeness that our actions prevent.

As a therapist, the lesson of Hoss was not lost on me. Good therapists are, by nature, playful—and good play is, by nature, therapeutic. I felt very fortunate to have been reminded of this so quickly after the tragedy, not only for my son's sake, but also for my own. While trauma and threat tend to take away the desire for playfulness, they intensify the need for it. To live through uncertain times, we cannot exist solely in a state of apprehension. It was not for nothing that Mayor Giuliani embraced the Yankees with such a childlike enthusiasm during the months that followed the attack.

Play is one of those things, like dreaming, that seems superfluous but that we cannot seem to live without. Like dreaming, play is driven by desire. It is a naturally arising, spontaneous expression of the self's need to negotiate all kinds of threatening situations, situations that throw a person into a confrontation with his own aloneness. As my son's discussions with Hoss made clear, successful play reveals both the truth *and* the falseness of these threats—they become trauma only when there is no way out. While it cannot be forced, play does seem to happen on its own, of its own accord, if the circumstances are right enough and if people are willing to put their agendas on hold. Its spirit emerges. Creative playing arises naturally out of a relaxed state. It opens up when a child knows that the parent is still present but in the background, available but not interfering, supportive but not making demands.

In the model that I am describing, play is the child's natural means of coping with disconnections that threaten, but do not actually become, trauma. In that sense, it is a template for what is possible when desire comes up against the gap between satisfaction and fulfillment. Rather than retreating in frustration or reacting with anger, there is another alternative that we have known since childhood.

In the midst of uncertainty, or in the face of disaster, we may be tempted to sacrifice our more playful sides. It is certainly, all too often, one of the more unfortunate casualties of "growing up." Part of the charm of Jack Engler's memories of India lies in Munindra's deft handling of Jack's seriousness of purpose. In his creation of a facilitating environment, Munindra reintroduced Jack to his playful nature, just as my son reminded me of mine. As we learn, through the dharma, to create this environment for ourselves, we can open more and more to a desire that is simple and easy: one that does not need to cling or control but that can constantly be surprised. As the Buddha's teachings never tire of pointing out, sometimes less is really more.

9

The Fruit

The Buddha's path is one that trains the mind to do the unexpected. It does this by teaching us how to willingly enter a non-purposive state in which "doing" and "being done to" give way to the simpler joy of "being." The Buddha was very clear about how this approach differed from the conventional one. "It goes against the stream," he commented in the first moments after his enlightenment. "Others will not understand me. That will be wearying and troublesome for me."[1] Yet the Buddha managed to find a way out of his predicament. He came up with a method that succeeded in grabbing people's attention. In its purest form it involved doing nothing: sitting in solitary meditation without being manipulated by likes and dislikes. But this "nothing" was far from uninspiring. Unlike almost all the world's other great religions, Buddhism moved from culture to culture solely by virtue of its ideas, never by way of conquering armies. The promise that it offered, relief from suffering by learning the art of not clinging, made enough sense that people of enormously varying backgrounds and cultures were willing to give it a try.

The interesting thing about his method is that, while it is often practiced in solitary meditation, it does not need to be. It can also be practiced in the world. It does not require us to give up our desires, only to turn our attention to them in an honest way. In its formulation of the left-handed path, Buddhism goes out of its way to show that the most sensual of desires can be recruited into practice. Even the sexual act can be used to train the mind.

RESISTANCE

As this possibility has filtered into popular consciousness, it has sometimes been put to defensive uses, not just spiritual ones. The mind, as we have seen, can cling to anything, even to concepts of non-clinging. I have heard a number of stories in my therapy practice, for instance, about men who abstain from ejaculating during sex. Under the guise of tantric sexuality, these men withdraw from sexual relations after some period of intercourse, leaving their lovers dissatisfied or believing they are inadequate. Their partners, rather than being uplifted, feel let down.

A patient of mine named Bob, for example, was an appealing man with a winning smile who was a great devotee of female beauty and charm, but he was something of a tease with women. He gave the impression of wholehearted interest when he met someone he was attracted to, but he would often disappear if she too obviously returned his attentions. He puzzled many would-be lovers with his skittishness. Married once in his twenties, Bob was now a successful physician in his mid-forties. He had been single for close to twenty years, and had become a proficient golfer. He lived a quiet, self-contained life and was much attracted to the philosophies of yoga and meditation.

In his sexual relations, Bob often took a rather tortuous path. He would initiate sex, participate for a while, but then refrain from orgasm, explaining his actions in terms of sexual yoga. I was suspicious, however. I did not hear reports of resounding bliss, only what sounded like gradual disengagement. I confronted him about this, reflecting on what I knew of the left-handed path. From what I could tell, I told Bob, the key thing about sexual yoga was the willingness to renounce grasping while in the midst of intense desire, without abandoning eros altogether. This ability, which is another way of describing the yielding of the masculine object-seeking mode to the feminine one of simply being, is meant to open up the possibility of the "shared contemplation" of yogic union.[2] This affords a rapport in which, in yogic language, the energies, breath and fluids of each partner mix to such an extent that blissful states are achieved that would otherwise remain inaccessible to an individual practitioner.

"Are you experiencing this kind of mutuality?" I asked Bob. He was not. In fact, it was quite the opposite. Feeling guilty about his unreliability, Bob tried to avoid getting any of his girlfriends too attached to him.

"I don't want them to see what a cad I am," he admitted.

I pointed out that this was exactly what they were seeing.

OPEN TO DESIRE

Bob believed in romantic love, and was disappointed over the failure of his first marriage, but in a reversal of the model of courtly love that is one basis for our notions of romance, Bob made himself into a receding object of desire. His girlfriends were like medieval knights questing after his ever-dissolving affections. Bob abandoned the role of the pursuer, but did not free himself from the entire schema. He simply made himself into the pursued object.

But this flip on the traditional mode of relating was not enough to break through to tantra. Bob and his lovers were not enjoying their desire, nor were they obtaining satisfaction. And *Bob's* desire was nowhere to be found. As we talked about all of this, Bob saw how much he blamed himself for the inevitable demise of his first marriage. He had not really let go of his ex-wife, or at least not of his feelings of failure in the marriage. His incomplete mourning interfered with his ability to give himself over to more current passions. His tantra was not really tantra. Rather than opening himself and his partner to unexplored states of mutual awareness, Bob hung on to one particular state of arousal, the one in which he was the object. He hid himself within that state, under the guise of being a sexual yogi, never allowing himself or his partners to enter more fertile areas of erotic intimacy where two subjects explore each other's ungraspable natures. In some ways, he was like a person addicted to peaceful meditation. He found solace in his ability to prolong his arousal, just as many meditators take comfort in their self-induced relaxation. But he was stuck there, using notions of sexual yoga to limit his engagement.

There is an old saying in Tibet that Tsoknyi Rinpoche quoted at a recent retreat. He was addressing a common issue in

164

meditation—of people becoming attached to their techniques—
but his point could just as easily apply to dynamics like Bob's.

"Just as the waters in the high mountains improve by falling," he said, "so do a yogi's meditations improve by dissolving."

Even in states of very refined meditative absorption, the saying implies, a version of self can persist in objectified form.
Somewhere within the meditator's consciousness he is still apt
to be thinking, "Oh, what a good yogi am I." Thus, his meditation could improve by dissolving. The self needs to flow, not to
be stuck. The same might be said of certain yogis' erections.
They, too, can improve by dissolving. Clinging to any state, no
matter how idealized, only perpetuates suffering.

THE DESIRE OF THE OTHER

In contrast to the more well-known paths of renunciation and
asceticism, the path of sensual awakening—the left-handed
path—takes ordinary passion and uses it to develop the mind in
a manner analogous to what can occur in solitary meditation.
First, the passionate yearning of erotic desire is used to develop
an expanded personal inner life, just as the more solitary introspection of classical meditation can do. This is done by intro-
ducing a person to the gap between satisfaction and fulfillment,
and encouraging him or her to enter that space instead of avoiding it. This promotes a confrontation with clinging and the realization that there is a limit to how much possession or control is
possible. The "objective" nature of reality starts to break down.
Objects become subjects, a process that is facilitated by the ex-
amination of clinging. This is what Bob may have been resisting. Rather than opening to the subjective experience of his

lover, he retreated into his own fear. Rather than using the erotic encounter as a window into the ephemeral nature of self and other, he closed himself off from his lover's experience.

But the secret teachings of the left-handed path counsel the opposite approach. By opening to the ineffable desire of the other, they suggest, we can go beyond subject and object altogether, sensing the ultimate ground of reality—called "emptiness"—in the midst of pleasurable experiences. Whether it is approached through solitary meditation or sensual desire, the highest yoga of Buddhist meditation involves mingling bliss and emptiness in an experience known as non-duality.

As this approach was spelled out in the deliberately elusive language of the tantras, it was, in effect, written on the body of the woman. Whether this was because the culture of medieval Buddhism was male dominated and so the female perspective represented the unknown "other," or because female desire actually holds a critically important secret, I do not know. But female imagery is all-pervasive in the literature of the left-handed path. Always intended as a secret language, the widespread use of such imagery was meant to be decipherable only to those who had been initiated onto the path. But as we read it, the unmistakable allure of the shared contemplation of the erotic couple can be felt. The female desire for release from object status is loud and clear. And this desire is valued as the foundation for the liberating wisdom that we all crave.

The appreciation of a woman's perspective on desire became so important in the secret mystical teachings of Tibet that it was a requirement in the dominant sect of Tibetan Buddhism for the most accomplished celibate monks to take a lover at some point in their practice in order to bring their minds into contact with it. The point of such lovemaking was not just to open up a forbidden sensual experience for meditative contemplation (although this was undoubtedly part of it), it was to put the mind of the meditator (usually male) in contact with the ungraspable bliss of female sensuality. The French philosopher Daniel Charles has described this sensuality as like that of a rice paddy.[3] In a rice paddy, each shoot of rice makes its own subterranean connection to an underground lattice composed of every other shoot. Instead of coalescing into one huge tuber (like a phallus), the rhizomes of a rice field form a matrix through which they all connect. Desire is dispersed, but held in a subterranean net whose overall vitality is nourishing for the whole. While male sexuality is like a vertical thrust, a woman's can become all-pervasive.

A RIVERBANK

One of the most renowned leaders and philosophers in the history of Tibet, the fourteenth-century reformer Je Tsong Khapa, was said to have passed up the opportunity to take a lover as part of his advanced meditative pursuits. He did not feel that his fellow monks were ready to understand, and so he chose to defer his lovemaking to another lifetime. In his day, this was quite an enormous sacrifice, because it was assumed that sexual intercourse was the most direct method of gaining a glimpse of nirvana. Nevertheless, his commentary on the *Cakrasamvaratantra* shows an appreciation of the liberating aspect of female sensuality and the ways in which this sensuality is equated with the birth of the subject.

In an initial read, as was probably intended by its authors, these sensual qualities are nowhere to be found. The tantra seems to be a relatively straightforward description of the rites and rituals of esoteric practice. In its first chapter, would-be practitioners are given instructions about how to draw a sacred mandala, a circle within which the transformational meditative processes can unfold:

> Draw the mandala on a mountain,
> In a medicinal valley or forest,
> Near the bank of a large river,
> Or in a primordial cremation ground.

The instructions do not seem at all ambiguous. One is tempted to rush through them without paying too much attention. Yet Tsong Khapa unpacked their secret meaning in his commentary. While he did not explicitly use the metaphor of the rice field, he came pretty close. The mandala, he made clear, was to be drawn on a woman's desire. All the metaphors, the mountain, the medicine, the valley, the forest, the riverbank and the cremation ground, refer to the infinite reach of a woman's sensual delight.

> Because her great bliss is imperturbable,
> She is a mountain.
> Because lesser beings cannot fathom her profundity,
> She is a forest.
> Because her cavern is filled with nectar,
> She is a cave.
> Because her union of wisdom and skill is deep,
> She is a riverbank.
> Because she [knows] the natural state beyond birth and death,
> She is primordial.
> Because she is the object of great bliss,

Her activity is natural.
Because she burns the views of early disciples and solitary
    achievers in the fire of great passion,
She is a cremation ground.[4]

In Tsong Khapa's verse, the first thing to become apparent is his intense idealization of the woman. Familiar enough to anyone who has fallen in love, his hyperbole reminds us of the "spell" that can fall over someone entranced by erotic desire. But Tsong Khapa's intent was to go further. The "object" cannot live up to the idealization of romantic love—it has to disappoint at some point in time. What saves us is the ungraspable nature of the subject, the ineffable otherness of the lover to whom one cannot cling. In Tsong Khapa's commentary, the metaphor for this was his lover's vastness.

The mandala in which awakening unfolds, Tsong Khapa made clear, is the interpersonal expanse created by a woman's desire. It is redolent throughout this verse. In the ecstatic feelings that are most commonly associated with erotic experience we can also find the bliss that is available in meditation. In Buddhist terms, this is the bliss that comes when we see the emptiness of self. Erotic experiences capture our imagination because they provide a glimpse of this reality. Under the spell of passion, both self and other dissolve. And it is female sexuality, with its intrinsic regard for spaciousness, its dispersal of desire over the entire body, and its valorization of the subjective voice, that holds the key. The esoteric Buddhist teachings suggest that when we bring attention to this kind of desire, it will teach us what the Buddha wanted us to understand.

Tsong Khapa detailed some of what can be known, or not known, as a result. He described not only an erotically charged interchange, but also a liberating state of consciousness. He took the male, object-based mode of desire—the same desire that Jack Engler displayed in his search for the dharma—and exploded it on the body of a woman. Her bliss, he declared right off the bat, is imperturbable; it cannot be touched. Her profundity cannot be fathomed. She cannot be controlled, possessed or contained, nor can she be approached in the usual manner. Her "primordial" quality, "beyond birth and death," is a consciousness not split by an object-based mode of perception.

The passion of an erotic relationship, once the female perspective is included, is capable of burning our usual object-based mode of thought. Just as Shiva burned Kama but then resurrected him, this passion can resurrect desire in a new, more spacious, mode. In a twist that Freud might have appreciated, the female perspective on desire is seen as ultimately liberating. Embracing it gives a peek into the underlying and fundamental nature of reality, from whence we all spring.

GRACE

The teachings of the sexual tantras all come down to one point. Although desire, of whatever shape or form, seeks completion, there is another kind of union than the one we imagine. In this union, achieved when the egocentric mode of dualistic thinking is no longer dominant, *we* are not united with *it*, nor am *I* united with *you*, but we all just are. The movement from object to subject, as described in both Eastern meditation and modern psychotherapy, is training for this union, but its perception usually comes as a surprise, even when this shift is well under way. It is a kind of grace. The emphasis on sexual relations in the tantric teachings makes it clear that the ecstatic surprise of orgasm is the best approximation of this grace. But it can happen at any moment, since it is happening in all of them. It is only our conventional way of thinking that hides it from us.

Both love relations and solitary meditation encourage this breakthrough by undercutting our usual ways of relating. They do this by engaging us in the pursuit of the impossible. In love, we pursue the Other, only to find that he or she is inaccessible, while in meditation we pursue the self, only to find it equally ineffable. Yet sometimes, unpredictably, in the midst of these pursuits, when the balance in the mind is right, an experience that we designate as oneness jumps out. But even this designation is problematic. Oneness implies the existence of twoness or threeness, but this experience says otherwise. It points instead to the presence of that which underlies the world of duality, to a union that is already present, not one that has to be achieved. It gives us a sense of completion, not by making a new whole but by exposing a mirage. It undercuts our notions of self and other, subject and object, and observer and observed. While it does not contradict the conventional experience, it puts it in perspective as only relatively real.

At its best, desire has the capacity to reveal the underlying nature of reality, to help us discover our natural state. That is why I believe Kasyapa smiled when the Buddha held up his flower. The natural state is not something that can be turned into an object, nor can it be found when we are searching for it *as* an object; it can only be experienced through the medium of personal experience. The words and symbols that are used to evoke or describe it might be helpful as far as they go, but they come after the fact and they do not go very far. At their peak, they give a sense of the flavor of some hidden capacity of the self: the capacity to know without resorting to objectification.

In its wisdom aspect, the natural state is said to be luminous and knowing; indefinable and indescribable; clear, unwavering, fertile and empty; ungraspable by language or conceptual thought. In the hidden erotic language of Tibetan Buddhism, the bliss of the Other is its most perfect expression. It is what desire is seeking but does not know how to regard.

Meditation, like desire, opens up inner life. The mind is trained to observe its usual object-based mode of operation ("I want this, I don't want that"), but this very training in self-observation deepens the capacity for individuality. It gives dimensionality to the self. Sooner or later, one begins to notice experiences that "are not ordered by language, concepts, or emotional response."[5] The more the inner life opens up, the more mysterious it becomes. If we were to try to phrase the questions that can bring us to this point, they would sound something like these: "I am sitting observing my own mind. Who is observing and who is being observed? I see that there is always an awareness, a consciousness, present. Is this me? But the I who is conscious of this awareness is different from awareness itself. Where are the boundaries of my self?" The more one is able to define the problem, the less sure one can possibly be. The process is one of a gradual surrender of what is called "dualistic thinking," the separation of experience into observer and observed, or subject and object. Ultimately, there is nothing to do but give up.

THE SUBJECT OF AWARENESS

The Buddhist psychologist Jack Engler, in a remarkable bit of writing about the changing nature of self experience in meditation, describes the approach to non-duality with an elegant specificity.[6] He is the same man whose teacher, Munindra, would at first talk to him only about the state of his bowels. But something more must have unfolded in Engler's meditations, for he takes a very confusing concept and makes it understandable in his writing. By opening the field of awareness to include all of the objects of mind and body, he notes, a meditator eventually has to confront the confounding problem of the source of awareness. There is nothing quite so vexing as trying to observe consciousness as it arises. As Engler correctly points out, in Freud's descriptions of the psychoanalytic method he was clear about the ego's ability to take itself as an object. In a famous statement, Freud described the ego as follows: "It can treat itself like any other object, observe itself, criticize itself, do heaven knows what besides with itself."[7] But Engler reveals an important, yet overlooked, corollary: The ego can never successfully take itself as the *subject* of awareness.

What does he mean? It is the essential realization of the left-handed path. Subjectivity can never be entirely known. To try to know it turns it into an object and strips it of its subjective quality. The only way to know it is to be it. This is where the lessons of desire start to manifest in the personal realm. While we tend to pursue our lovers as objects, we are quickly washed up on the shores of their subjectivity. And just as we cannot locate or possess their subjectivity, we cannot completely know our own. In love relations we find that our lovers are out of reach but we can learn to bask in their otherness, in the interpersonal expanse that female sexuality makes possible. In meditation we find that our own awareness is similarly always eluding us, and the solution is parallel. Like a skilled lover, as awareness opens it also evades. To know it, we have to give up trying to tie it down. Listen to Engler's description of his meditative experiences:

*"Whatever I can be aware of, whatever I notice or conceptu-
alize, whether in the field of sense perception or intrapsychically,
is always an object of my awareness—never awareness itself. I
can become aware of being aware, but when this happens, what I
have done is take this reflexive awareness as an object of experience. What I cannot do is be aware of the source of awareness in
the act of being aware. In other words, I cannot directly observe
my observing self. If I try, it recedes each time I turn to observe it:
I never catch 'it'; I only turn the act of awareness into another
object of awareness in an infinite regression."*[8]

While Engler's point may seem difficult, for anyone who
has ever tried to meditate it is not hard to understand. Whatever we become aware of automatically becomes an "object,"
just as it does when we try to make a sentence out of it. "I am
aware of *it*." No matter how hard we try, a sense of separation
between us and our experience is inevitable. The ego is always
split. But there are certain situations in which another mode of
perception bursts forth. As the tantric adepts describe, there are
moments when we stumble into a complete surrender of the
object-based relational mode, when we swim in the subjectivity of the other. The "non-dual" nature of things can then be
understood.

This is where the yoga of desire comes into play. The classical Tibetan Buddhist approach is to equate the "subjectless subjectivity" of the nature of mind with the unfathomable
otherness of a lover. This is all conflated into a female deity
called a *dakini*. Literally translated as a "traveler in space," or a
"sky-dancer," the *dakini*, whose erotic form mirrors the early
Indian fertility goddesses seen ringing the first Buddhist stupas,

represents the mind when it is understood as "no object of any kind."[9]

The veteran Tibetan lama Chogyam Trungpa once gave a good response when asked the question, "What are *dakinis*?"

"One never knows," he replied, signaling their true meaning.[10]

In the symbolic view, when a yogi discovers the vast subjective expanse of his or her own mind and appreciates its objectless nature, this is equated with meeting the *dakini*. But the beauty of the tantric approach is that it is not only true in symbolic language, it can also be experienced in the real world. As the Buddhist scholar Jeffrey Hopkins explains in several books that he has written on the subject, Tibetan Buddhism is notoriously "sex-friendly." Walls of Tibetan temples are adorned with paintings of men and women in states of sexual arousal. The happiness that comes in lovemaking allows a couple to slip through a portal into the *dakini*'s domain.

Most portrayals of sexual yoga describe methods of making this state of consciousness accessible. The man is encouraged to give priority to his partner's arousal rather than his own. There is a deliberate enhancing of female excitement and a corresponding heightening of sensuality. Both partners are urged to bring pleasurable feelings upward from their genitals to fill the rest of the body, prolonging their intermingling while allowing sexual bliss to course through mind and body. In a reversal of the usual sexual dynamic, men are urged to absorb the female secretions— to drink their bliss—rather than just ejaculate. All of this is in the service of opening up the sensual, intersubjective mode of relating, using genital pleasure as a foundation for shared contemplation rather than as an end in itself.

FOR WANT OF DESIRE

In a recent book, Adam Phillips wrote of Freud's discussions of desire in a way that suggested that Freud knew more of tantra than we might have suspected.[11] Phillips retold a story of Freud's from an often-overlooked paper called "On Transience." In this vignette, Freud told of walking in the countryside with two friends who were resolutely unmoved by the beauty of all that surrounded them. Freud was puzzled by their failure to open and began to analyze what their problem might be. Their hearts were closed, their desire lacking, but he could not at first figure out why. Freud's entire discussion might be read, in fact, as a tantric teaching, played out in the countryside of the Austrian Alps. It is as if he were drawing the sacred mandala that Tsong Khapa wrote about centuries before.

After some reflection, he came up with an explanation for his companions' mental state. It was the transience of the physical world that was unnerving his friends, he decided. They were guarding themselves against a feeling of sadness that was an indivisible part of appreciation. Like a lover who has been hurt one too many times, Freud's friends were keeping themselves unapproachable, avoiding the emotional surrender that the scene called for because of nature's ultimate unreliability. They were stuck in a state of abbreviated, or interrupted, mourning. Unwilling to embrace the world in all of its ephemerality, they retreated to a sullen and unapproachable place. Freud was incredulous at this. "It was incomprehensible, I declared, that the thought of the transience of beauty should interfere with our joy in it . . . A flower that blossoms for a single night does not seem to us on that account less lovely."[12]

But Freud was soon persuaded that his friends' reactions were not an anomaly. As Phillips concluded, in a deft twist of a phrase, there seem to be two kinds of people in the world, "those who can enjoy desiring and those who need satisfaction."[13] One clings and the other doesn't. Freud's companions were definitely of the school that needed satisfaction; but Freud, the apostle of instinctual gratification, was someone who could understand the enjoyment of desire. This distinction lies at the heart of sexual tantra. Like Freud's friends, most of us are conditioned to look for fulfillment for our desire. When it is not forthcoming, or not lasting, we tend to withdraw. Rather than rejoice in our lovers' evasion of our attempts to control them, we feel dejected. In the face of unreliability, we retreat into our known selves. Our mourning paralyzes us, and our desire gets derailed. Freud proposed an alternative, one that in the East is personified in the path of desire. It is possible to be in a state in which desire is valued, not as a prelude to possession, control or merger but as a mode of appreciation in itself. "Doing," as Winnicott would say, becomes balanced by "being."

Freud's friends resisted "being" because it was too redolent of impermanence for them. For want of desire, they stayed aloof. They preferred the permanence of an incomplete mourning to the transience of a world that moved them but made them afraid. But Freud, unaware of the Buddhist flavor of the insight he was tapping into, knew that this conundrum could only be solved by stepping back into a more appreciative mode. The "smiling countryside" of Freud's summer sojourn washed an ocean of feelings over him. Transience, longing, reverence and mourning were all of a piece. It was Freud, not chasing satisfaction, who could stay present with it all. Worlds away from the high mountains of the Himalayas, his observations in the Alps nevertheless bore out the old Tibetan saying: "Just as the waters in the high mountains improve by falling, so do a yogi's meditations improve by dissolving." By opening to desire, Freud found, the mind, like the high mountain water, also takes a plunge. Having fallen, it can flow through all things.

·IV·

A PATH
FOR DESIRE

You are Narayana who moves on the waters.

You flow through us all. You are Rama and Sita

born out of Earth and Ravana the Demon King,

you are Hanuman like the wind, you are

Lakshmana like a mirror, you are Indrajit and

Indra, you are the Poet and the Players and the

Play. And born as a man you forget this, you lose

the memory, and take on man's ignorance again,

as you will, every time.

Therefore, welcome back your Sita. The war

is done, and so we close our letter.

Ramayana *(p. 351)*

10

Advice

While some might think the opposite, it is desire that leads to the end of clinging. In both Western psychoanalysis and Eastern tantra, this path is spelled out in remarkably similar terms. Desire, which starts out wanting to control, possess, merge with or otherwise *do something* to or with an object, eventually finds that the object is not object enough for its liking. At this point, there is a fork in the road. In one direction lies clinging, the attempt to make the object more than it can be; and in the other direction lies non-clinging, where the gap between what is expected and what is actually found can be tolerated. This second direction—the left-handed path—requires a shift in consciousness and a training of the mind. It does not come naturally. The training is described in both East and West as enabling a progression from "doing" to "being," "male" to "female," and "object" to "subject." This development does not negate the importance of the active, masculine, object-seeking type of desire, but it does balance it out so that the world is no longer approached from a single vantage point with a single strategy.

In opening up this alternative strategy, we enter the less familiar territory of an intuitive knowing that is only possible once we learn to discipline our own minds. Desire, in this way of thinking, becomes its own yoga. Its very arising makes it possible to train our minds to work differently. In an apocryphal statement attributed to James Joyce, he once described the attention that is necessary to look at a work of art as "beholding." If the viewer gets too close to an artwork it becomes pornography or if he gets too distant it becomes criticism. Beholding art means giving it enough space to let it speak to us, to let us find it, even if we do not completely understand what we are looking at. The left-handed path opens up this capacity for beholding. When we discover that the object is beyond our control, unpossessable and receding from our grasp, we have the opportunity to enter the space that Joyce was referring to. When we take the left-handed path, we learn to give the object its freedom.

The kind of desire that the psychoanalysts have gendered as feminine speaks of this Joycean beholding. We seek it in both spiritual and sexual life. The paradox is that it can only be found by allowing desire to function in its aggressive, object-seeking, "masculine" way. It is this very drive that awakens the mind to the impossibility of its demands, that pushes it to explore the uncharted territory of its own dissatisfaction. The path of desire requires an acceptance of, and a confrontation with, the truth of our own longings. The fruit of this confrontation is the successful mingling of the two energies, a union that reveals the taste of non-duality.

The copulating figures that adorn much of Tibetan art represent the interpenetration or intermingling of the male and female approaches. In this tradition the active male desire, chastened by the gap that desire creates, becomes empathy or compassion: the ability to reach into the experience of another and feel what they are feeling. The desire to possess or control becomes the ability to relate. The beholding desire, represented by the female partner, is a metaphor for wisdom, as exemplified by the capacity to be. This formulation has always impressed me because it reverses the conditioned way of thinking. Compassion is male and wisdom female.

PRINCIPLES OF THE PATH

The Buddha's Eightfold Path, his Fourth Noble Truth, described the way to make desire into its own path, to turn it from clinging to non-clinging. In so doing, the Fourth Noble Truth showed how to balance doing with being so that we can experience the bliss that the copulating figures of wisdom and compassion suggest. In the Buddhist view, this is the "higher" bliss that desire seeks. While the Path is traditionally described in a list of eight "Right" categories: the behavioral or ethical foundation of Right Speech, Right Action and Right Livelihood; the meditative foundation of Right Concentration, Right Effort and Right Mindfulness; and the wisdom foundation of Right Understanding and Right Thought, it can also be talked about in more conventional language. When dealing with the real world, it can be helpful to have some basic principles to work with, reminders of how to use desire to open up our understanding, and open up ourselves.

While the esoteric knowledge of how to use erotic desire to bring the mind into a state of non-clinging has always been shrouded in secrecy, the basic principles, while at times counterintuitive, are not hard to appreciate. The beauty of the tantric approach, after all, is that it can be used in the midst of our regular lives. But to make use of it requires a juggling of our usual ways of approaching things. We have to challenge the fundamental orientation that we have in the world as we try to make sense of our place in it: the tendency to identify with our own experience and to separate self from other. We have to find a way to move ourselves out of an exclusive identification with our own thoughts. In this light, the first principle of the journey is to learn to see desire as impersonal.

It has become a fundamental axiom of our culture that we have to "take responsibility" for our emotions, just as we must for our physical health. But it is interesting that Freud's own strategy for working with emotions took exactly the opposite tack. In his own way, Freud discovered anew what Buddhists had practiced for millennia, that the first step in healing our relationship to desire is seeing it as not self. In treating patients who were completely out of touch with the nature of their erotic strivings, Freud repeatedly instructed them in a fundamental truth about desire's nature.

"We are not responsible for our feelings," he would tell them, emphasizing how important it was for them to change their emotional stance toward their desire.[1] I remember hearing almost the same thing from Joseph Goldstein, my Buddhist meditation instructor, at one of my first retreats. "It's not *what* is happening in your mind that matters," he would say, "it's how you relate to it." Freud noted how difficult it was for his patients to accept the reality of sexual feelings they were not proud of, and how that refusal transformed their feelings into neurotic symptoms. In his famous case study of Little Hans, for example, he showed how the young boy, a patient of his in 1909 who developed crippling anxiety over horses after a bad fall, was actually afraid of his own sexual and aggressive urges toward his mother and father. Hans transferred these fears to the horse and then became more and more afraid. Only by unpacking these kinds of fears could Freud be of help. His patients held themselves *too* responsible for their desires, and were too judgmental of themselves as a result. In order to get them to accept their feelings, Freud found it necessary to teach his patients how to not identify with them so much. The paradox of this is interesting. Freud's patients suffered from estrangement from vital aspects of themselves. But they could not harness the energy of their desire and aggression until they could accept the impersonal nature of those very feelings. Healing could only take place if the self was willing to relinquish ownership of its contents.

This strategy of Freud's is pivotal to understand, because it upends the conventional view, even among many therapists, of what the therapeutic task should be. Yet it is entirely consistent with the Buddha's left-handed path, in which a crucial strategy is the willingness to not take the contents of the psyche too personally. While the acceptance of desire is certainly essential to deepen the experience of self, it is not necessary to assume that this desire is "ours." It is easier to accept if we see it as coming from a mysterious place. This is the original meaning of the words that Freud used for the unconscious, what we have come to call, in English, the *id*. The German words, *das es*, that Freud actually used, translate as *the it*. The unconscious always seemed like a ruthless and impersonal "Other" to Freud.

I once read a *New York Times Magazine* interview with a well-known Jungian psychotherapist that went one step further. James Hillman, probably the most accomplished contemporary American descendant of Jung, took a position that was completely consistent with this impersonal view while drawing out its implications. Rather than stopping at Freud's use of "the it," Hillman tried to get at the subjective expanse that desire holds within.

> *"Most theoretical models hold that rages, fears and passions are our personal responsibility," Hillman was quoted as saying. "Somehow, somewhere, they are located inside of us. . . . My contention here, however, shall be that though they be felt deeply, and we suffer emotions physically and inwardly, this fact does not make them 'ours.' Rather, I believe that emotions are there to make us theirs. They want to possess us, rule us, win us over completely to their vision."*

Hillman was drawing from ancient mythology in his statement, and some would call his point of view naive or childlike. From a certain analytic perspective, seeing the emotions as like the gods of old involves the defense of projection, in which essential aspects of the self are dissociated into external forces that are then experienced as outside of our control. But Hillman was suggesting that there is more wisdom than projection in the ancient view. Emotions *are* like the gods of the old world, linking us to our souls. When we repress them, we are totally cut off, and stuck in our impoverished selves. But when we identify completely with the emotions, when we think that they are us, we are letting the gods trick us. In either case, in repression or in possession, we lose the capacity for wonder that our emotional lives make possible. Desire is one means of keeping us in contact with this wonder.

Seeing desire as having its own agenda frees us to look at it more evenly. As Sappho observed so many years ago, it comes from elsewhere, stirs us up, makes us question who exactly is in charge, and carries the possibility of enrichment as well as the threat of obsession. From this perspective, the arising of desire becomes an opportunity to question, not *what* we desire, nor what we *do* with desire, nor even how we make *sense* out of desire, but what does desire want from us? What is its teaching? We have to be very quiet to listen to desire in this way.

THREADS OF BLUE

The next principle of working with desire is to see it as divine. By this, I do not mean simply idealizing the beloved in the manner common in early stages of falling in love, although this is an eye-opening experience in itself. I mean the recognition of how incredible it is to be capable of desiring, or being desired, in the first place. Especially when stripped of all the addictive fixations that can accrue, the mere existence of desire as an energy that can enthuse us is awe inspiring. The recognition of the divine in desire is less about moving toward an ideal than it is about acknowledging its immanence.[2] The American psychoanalyst James Grotstein has pioneered this particular approach, writing persuasively about "the sacred architecture of the psyche," rescuing us from the prejudice that the unconscious is primitive and "less than human." Rather than seeing it in this way, Grotstein has stressed the "loftiness, sophistication, versatility, profundity, virtuosity and brilliance that utterly dwarf the conscious aspects of the ego."[3] Like Winnicott, he has also emphasized the unfathomable aspects of the subjective self, but he has a way of formulating it that is especially relevant to the lessons of Indian philosophy. The unconscious, particularly the ineffable subject, is like a god, Grotstein has written, "but a handicapped one, because it needs partners in order for its mission to be completed."[4] As in the *Ramayana*, where gods and animals have to work together to discover the intersubjective expanse of what it means to be human, we need partners in order to realize who we are. While psychotherapy and meditation offer reliable venues for this exploration, our love relations do also.

In the holiest prayer of the Jewish tradition, the *Sh'ma*, there is a beautiful verse about how changing one's perspective on desire opens up its enlightening potential. Originating in the context of Moses's revelations on Mt. Sinai, this verse explains how Moses was instructed to turn desire from something that kept him away from God to something that reminded him of God's blessings. It was, in essence, a way of pulling Moses out of his ego-based identification with desire, into a more reflective consciousness that permitted an appreciation of God in the everyday world of mind and body. It was another way of opening up his mind, taking something that he assumed was "his" and making him think about it in another way. The complete verse is as follows:

> *God said to Moses:*
> *Let Israel throughout her generations make* tzitzit
> *Fringes, with a thread of blue,*
> *On the corners of her garments*

To look at and remember all the mitzvot* *of God*
And do them.

Otherwise
All of you will follow only what your eyes see
And your heart's desire,
Forgetting that everything you see
And whatever you desire
Are signs of My presence in the world.

But looking at the knotted fringes
You will remember as a knot around the finger
That everything you see
And whatever you desire
Can be seen and done
As one of my mitzvot.

Thus will you share the holiness of God
Who saw you as slaves in Egypt
And desired you
To become a people of God.[5]

The double-edged nature of desire is readily apparent in this remarkable verse. If left on his own, Moses was told, he would identify too much with his desires; he would follow only what he saw and what he longed for, without any thought of what was beyond. He would, in the language of the Bible, be a slave to his desires, or in the language of Buddhism, be tricked by the

*blessings

illusion of them. But God clearly wanted Moses to understand that desire was capable of more than that. Not only could his desire remind him of the presence of God, but God, too, had a desire: that Moses remember him. In the meeting of the two desires, a new experience was possible.

God gave Moses several meditative practices to turn his mind around. Not only did he tell him to weave blue threads into his garments, the way an Indian yogi might finger a rosary of *mala* beads to keep his mind on God, but he gave an even more explicit practice to Moses. This was imparted just before the verses quoted above, and sets the stage for these teachings. The first part of the *Sh'ma* is a lesson in meditation, a prayer whose deeper meaning is not often addressed in contemporary Judaism: "Hear, O Israel," it proclaims, "The Lord our God, the Lord is One."

Anyone who enters a synagogue hears this prayer; it is repeated in virtually every service that takes place there. I grew up hearing it but was never sure if the rabbi was saying "Here, O Israel" or "Hear, O Israel." Either way, the words passed through my head without ever making much of an impact. At most, I think, I tied it to the early Bible stories I had been told as a child about the golden calf and the Jewish people's tendency toward idolatry. Do not worship many gods, Moses was told, worship only one.

But the prayer is much deeper than that. Each word has a meaning that resonates. "Israel" itself means "He who struggles, or wrestles, with God." It is a name for anyone willing to confront the profoundly mysterious nature of our beings, for anyone who wonders where desire might actually lead. "Hear, O Israel," the prayer implores. "Hear," as in *listen to your own souls*. The prayer is an attempt to turn awareness in a spiritual direction, to listen in a deeper way than is usual, to cultivate the ardor, or *tapas*, that in India is directed into meditation. "Listen to your own souls, you who struggle with God," the *Sh'ma* proclaims. As in Buddhism, listening in a deep way, undistracted by the clamor of the mind, is essential to transform the experience of desire.

God is not separate, the prayer insists: *The Lord is One*. This flies in the face of the way desire ordinarily apprehends things—where there are always two. But the world of duality does not have to be accepted at face value. Everything we see and whatever we desire can be experienced as signs of God's presence. The blue threads, knotted to Moses's clothing, are visceral reminders of this truth, but our own desires can function in much the same way. They, too, are threads of blue, living representations of God's blessings. This is where the spiritual possibilities of desire begin to make sense. Just as the Indian cosmologies refuse to make a distinction between the microcosm and the macrocosm, between the erotic and the divine, so does the *Sh'ma* seem to indicate a similar linkage. By attending to desire with the same care that we might listen to our souls, we can move out of our usual way of thinking where there are always two: an observer and an observed. The *Sh'ma* points toward non-clinging, toward the *dakini*, toward the shared subjective reality where there is no object of any kind.

Freud taught his patients to disidentify from their conflicted desires to get them over their shame and aversion to themselves. God taught Moses to disidentify from more acceptable desires by cultivating the knowledge that they were signs of His beneficence. The Dalai Lama described a similar practice in Tibetan Buddhism of using the appearances of the phenomenal world as a means of knowing "emptiness." He compared the knowledge of someone who understands emptiness to a person wearing sunglasses. The very appearance of the distorted color, he suggested, serves as a reminder that what is being seen is not real. In the Buddhist view, what is revealed is "emptiness," while in the Jewish view it is called *"Ein-Sof,"* the infinite. In classical Indian thought, one way that it is described is as the limitless shaft of Shiva's *lingam*, or phallus. Issues of idolatry aside, the three are closer in spirit than most people might think. Linking all of them is the understanding that bringing non-judgmental awareness to desire deepens its mystery.

By learning to see desire as more of an impersonal force, as happens under the spell of prayer, meditation or psychotherapy, the soul is invigorated. The links between desire and the divine are opened as the self's appropriation of desire is loosened. Like a knot around the finger, desire, ever present and often troubling, can serve as a vivid reminder of our connection to something vaster than our everyday minds.

In practice, it is easier to treat some kinds of desire as sacred than others. Examples of how difficult it can be to see the divinity of desire often come up in therapy. A patient of mine named Betty, for example, a successful dermatologist affiliated with an uptown medical school, used to willingly lend her lover colorful and expensive scarves from her drawers when her girlfriend needed something special to wear to work. Her lover always received comments about how good they looked—a result that made both Betty and her girlfriend happy and proud. One day, however, Betty's lover took a scarf without asking. Betty felt hurt and invaded and it caused a rift between them. The scarf was "hers," after all, Betty told me—she had a right to be upset. But her lover did not see it that way. She felt criticized when

Betty raised the issue, and a symbolic act, once sweet, now turned sour.

While my first impulse was to sympathize with Betty's outrage, I waited to see if there might be more to the story. I wondered why Betty, who was generally very levelheaded, would make such a big deal about protocol. She certainly seemed to be treating her lover's desire (not just for the scarf, but for all that it might represent) as less than divine. Betty's mother, it turns out, had always been critical of Betty's childhood desires for her. The story that was repeated in the family was that Betty would scream "till she was blue in the face" when she wanted comfort or attention, while her favored sister was placid, never demanding anything. Was Betty treating her lover the way her mother had treated her—ostracizing her because of how greedy she could be? Was the scarf drawer another version of her mother's (or her own) breast? Did her lover always have to ask before she could take from it?

I told Betty the story of the *Sh'ma*. What if she could see her lover's desire not only as selfish but also as divine? Wouldn't she want God to help herself to her scarves? The principle of seeing desire as divine helped Betty disengage from her unconscious identification with her mother's critical attitude. It opened up an exchange not restricted by measurement or manners, where every demand did not have to be experienced as a violation.

INDESTRUCTIBLE

The third principle of working with desire is to not be intimidated by anger, but to see it as inevitable. The psychoanalyst Michael Eigen, in a recent work entitled *Ecstasy*, meditates on what he learned from Winnicott about this principle. "When the destructiveness built into aliveness . . . comes flying at the mother, can the mother not retaliate?" he wonders. Eigen asks this question the way Winnicott did, implicitly assuming that the mother intuitively knows another way. "There is a moment when embracing [a] baby's energy is not the point, but not retaliating is. At such a moment, the caregiver or caretaker . . . is not long-suffering or striking back or resentful. Everything hinges on recognizing the destructive 'attack' for what it is, a spontaneous part of aliveness. The destructive momentum of aliveness is joined by a spontaneous act of recognition.

"This does not mean the mother subjects herself to chronic injury. It does mean she does not blow up imaginary injury and respond in moralistic, annihilating ways. It involves human beings evolving to the point where they make room for the destructive element that is part of the backcloth of relationships. It means making room for disturbing feelings."[6]

From an analytic perspective, the growth of empathy and compassion depends on how early experiences of anger, hatred and rage are met. Developmentally, the central task of the infant is to make sense out of the fact that he or she both loves and hates the same person. This is one of the most sobering experiences of parenthood, to find oneself the object of such an array of conflicting feelings. Winnicott used to say that a parent's task is simply to survive, not to retaliate and not to abandon in the face of a child's rage. Doing this "well enough" allows a child to come to terms with the reality of a parent as a separate individual, one who is outside of the child's control.

In Tibetan Buddhism, the aggressive desire of the male phallus, which, as feminist psychoanalysts like Jessica Benjamin have described, can often represent the wish to control, possess, dominate or objectify the other, is represented as the agent of compassion. Its role is completely transformed. While the Tibetans equate a woman's desire with the wisdom that understands emptiness, the male embodies compassion. The link with Winnicott's version of emotional development is interesting. When the mother makes room for the child's aggressive pursuit of her, he can learn that she survives his assault. Her otherness is established. Out of the pursuit of the object comes the recognition of the other, and out of the recognition of the other comes the capacity to empathize. The phallus pursues the object, but ultimately finds that it is unfindable. Yet rather than finding itself impotent, the phallus becomes an instrument of empathy. It can make a reparative gesture by caressing the loved one's otherness.

As Winnicott described, if the other's subjective self is never recognized, there can be no gesture of reconciliation, neither in the domain of infancy nor in erotic life. Tenderness can only be arrived at by successfully navigating anger's terrain. In infancy, it is the mother's responsibility to hold this anger, to not take it too personally. In erotic life, a second opportunity is given to experience the entire range of love and hate, converging on the body of another. While many couples are either frightened away by this prospect or are unable to contain each other's rage, the possibility is there to experience the empathy that comes from the survival of mutual destruction. Anger is what makes the beloved knowable in his or her subjectivity. It is a mistake to push too hard to eradicate it from our relationships.

One of my favorite passages in all of psychoanalytic literature is about this liberating quality of anger and the contradictory yearning of desire to both possess and release the loved object. The quotation, from a book called *Love Relations* by the psychoanalyst Otto Kernberg, speaks of the painful but joyous realization of the beloved's otherness that is brought about through an accepting attitude toward desire's frustration. Its language is a bit off-putting, but it succinctly describes how intimate sexual relations can bring us to a place of mystical knowledge, not through merger but through an opening up of the vastness that hangs between two individuals. The passage is about the painful yet liberating revelations of erotic love wherein the desire to possess one's lover comes up against the ineffability of their otherness. In its own unique way, it describes the path of desire as beautifully as the Indian myth of the *Ramayana*:

"... the beloved presents himself or herself simultaneously as a body which can be penetrated and a consciousness which is impenetrable. Love is the revelation of the other person's freedom. The contradictory nature of love is that desire aspires to be fulfilled by the destruction of the desired object, and love discovers that this object is indestructible and cannot be substituted."[7]

The most difficult aspect of this passage is its language of destruction, but it is precisely this aspect of desire that psychoanalysts have sought to understand and accept. Erotic love unites two streams: one that wants to take over the other to such a degree that it could devour or destroy it and another that wants to give it its freedom. Erotic desire is the physical attempt to reach the other, coupled with the intuition that they are forever out of reach. At times of greatest intimacy, both are felt simultaneously. It is out of this combination that empathy, compassion and consideration—as well as erotic bliss—emerge. In couples who try too hard to keep anger at bay, the first casualty is usually their erotic connection. By treating anger as *more* dangerous than the mother who knows it as a natural part of her child's aliveness, they annihilate the energy that is required to keep them seeking each other.

In the ruthless desire of lover for beloved are all of the early impulses of the child. Played out on the field of the body, but propelled by the archaic hungers of the mind, we pursue each other with the fervor of infants while dwelling in the bodies of men and women. And this is an indispensable aspect of erotic passion. But, just as in the Buddha's Noble Eightfold Path, there is an ethical dimension that comes into play when frustration is responded to properly. The urge to possess the object of desire does not disappear when the recognition of the other's separateness is achieved, but it becomes tempered by compassion. This is the source of the poignancy of Kernberg's statement. The revelation of the other person's freedom is a mixed blessing. Implicit in their freedom is the ultimate frustration of our quest to know them completely. There is always something left over. Kernberg identifies this all-important something as the other's consciousness. This is what remains hidden and out of reach, revealed only occasionally, like the rushing waterfall glimpsed through the trees of a Japanese garden.

Sexual life is a grand stage for this ongoing drama. At the same time as we seek to possess our lovers, we become equally conscious of their inviolability. The successful survival of the loved object is what turns it into a person. Sexual relations offer just this kind of revelation. On one level, they let us act out, over and over again, the passion of the infant and the survival of the mother. They let us treat each other as objects in a welcome relief from our everyday more civilized behavior. But erotic love can obviously do much more than that. When Winnicott wrote of the incommunicado element present in all of us, he was referring to the impenetrability of another's consciousness. Yet it is the great wonder of sexual relations that this other consciousness, foreign though it may be, opens itself to us at times.

As the final line in Kernberg's passage reminds us, "Love discovers that this object is indestructible and cannot be substituted." Impersonal, divine and astonishingly frustrating, desire takes us to a place we could never have anticipated, where the "object's" specialness is not tarnished by its refusal to cooperate.

11

Jumping In

The final principle of the yoga of desire is to stay still in the midst of it. On the Eightfold Path, this might be called Right Action or Right Effort, but it also embodies the principle of Right Mindfulness, in which equal attention is given to all moments of awareness without leapfrogging toward an end-point or goal. The willingness to proceed at such a deliberate pace is not something that we necessarily come to naturally; it often has to be enforced. At the meditation center where I sometimes engage in silent retreats, for example, the walking meditations are all done as if in slow motion. On beautiful spring days, the lawns and paths are littered with people walking back and forth slowly and steadily going nowhere. All the attention they can muster is in their feet: lifting, moving and placing one after the other. From afar, it looks as if it must be a mental hospital.

Yet the cultivation of this kind of attention is the key to the Eightfold Path. Within the domain of desire it is also the transformative element that catalyzes the emergence of a dormant sensibility. A patient of mine, an accomplished student of the Chinese martial art tai chi, gave me a good description of how threatening such a transformation can sometimes seem. He started to notice, after years of practicing his technique, how uncomfortable he became when, as they say in that world, his *chi* was flowing. While this state, of the energy of the body flowing uninterruptedly along the acupuncture meridians, was the fruition of his particular practice, something about it made my patient feel nervous.

Upon reflection, he found that it was uncharacteristic of him to savor any pleasurable experience, let alone this one, despite his self-image as a man ruled by desire. He noticed that he was always in a rush. He would prepare an elegant meal but then eat it so quickly that he developed stomach problems. He would look forward to an event but then be in a hurry to leave. He called this dynamic "jumping in," because his need for the next thing was always so intense that he would have to run right out of the last one without ever having had much of an experience. What he noticed in his tai chi practice was another example of this same phenomenon. He wanted to run away quickly from the very pleasure that he had worked so assiduously to achieve.

His comments reminded me of a time not long ago when I received some important instruction about the way out of "jumping in." This teaching came from what I thought then was an unlikely source. I was in Maine in the summertime, on a small island off Deer Isle where we rent an old house with no electricity for a week every summer. The island has only a few seasonal inhabitants; we have to bring all of our supplies by sea. It is as close to camping as we ever get as a family. Days there stretch from sunrise to sunset with only the early morning horn of the mailboat to remind us of civilization. The green of the island's interior is ringed by blue sea and sky. In the warm days of August, it is a glittering wonderland of sun, water, rocks and ocean breezes.

On one side of the island, down a path past an old tennis court lined with raspberry bushes, is a narrow cove, almost a fjord, that fills at high tide to a swimmable depth. The banks of this inlet are mudflats that heat up at low tide, warming the cold Atlantic waters as they flood past. If high tide comes in the early afternoon and the day is hot enough, we can swim there, an extremely rare occurrence in the freezing Maine ocean. When these circumstances come together, it is a cause for celebration. Most of the island's inhabitants, from the youngest child to the oldest elder, come to partake.

My tendency, like that of my patient, was to jump in and then rush very quickly to the shore. Even on the warmest days, the water, while tolerable, was still very cold. I would make a big deal about going in and then come running and splashing my way out. I liked it best when I was all alone there and I would often try to time things to be the first or the last at my favorite spot. Once when I came down for a swim, however, there was already another person in the water: a longtime summer resident named Margaret, probably in her sixties, although age is a difficult thing to judge on the island. She is a smart, elegant and hearty woman, a painter who had grown up spending long summers there and who often stayed on for weeks into the fall by herself. She is exquisitely in tune with the place. Like Sita, she has developed herself in isolation on an island. On this day though, I was not so aware of her profundity. While I admired her connection to the island, I never thought she was a repository of esoteric knowledge. I mostly thought of her as the woman from the house next door whose husband had battery-powered pruning shears that he wielded at odd hours.

Margaret was standing very still in the water, which was up about chest high. She noticed me noticing her and after a while she made a comment. "Inch by inch," she said, and she took a tiny step deeper into the sea. "I don't understand those people who go rushing in," she added sometime later.

I stayed on the bluff watching her, trying not to take her comment too personally. It was very peaceful. The sun was beating down and the water was gently lapping at the shore. Boats sailed far out in the distance. An osprey circled overhead, crying to its mate. I watched as Margaret moved imperceptibly into the water. Time passed.

"Aren't you cold?" I inquired finally. The water was just about up to her chin.

"You should try it," she murmured, before the ocean covered her mouth.

I edged myself down to the water and entered it one foot at a time. Standing ankle deep, I gasped at how cold it felt. To come in so quietly and slowly demanded much more courage than rushing in and out with my usual bravado. The more macho approach was actually a more fearful one. My feet quickly began to hurt and then to feel numb.

"Just wait," she called from far out in the cove. She was swimming now, but still watching me. "Wait till you get used to it, then come in a little more."

As I inched into the water, I began to notice how spectacular everything was. Hot above and cold below. But the cold was unusually comfortable. As the submerged parts of my body got used to it, it felt very easy to be there. And my upper body was full of the heat of the sun. My attention came to rest on the line between air and water. Each new step shifted the boundary a tiny bit upward, drawing a new circle around my torso. Certain moments were more difficult than others: when my hands first touched the water, when my groin went under, when my nipples were immersed and when my neck was touched. But each time the initial shock gave way to ease. It took about half an hour for the water to reach my mouth, but I still felt warm. The top of my head was radiant. I had never stayed in this water for longer than about four or five minutes. This was something else.

I managed to stay standing, even though the buoyancy of the ocean wanted to lift me away. I let the water move up my face, cover my eyes and wash over my forehead. Only the very top of my head was still open to the sky. From the inside, it reminded me of meditation. The bulk of my body was under the water, just as most of my experience could be observed mindfully in contemplation. But there was one piece that was still not engulfed, that reminded me of consciousness trying to observe itself. Most of me was in the water, but a little bit was still away. I was like desire reaching for its object, only to find it eluding me. Duality still held me in its sway.

Suddenly, I felt the ocean close over my scalp. Burning hot became oh so cool. I was submerged, and I lifted my feet off the muddy bottom and began to whirl under the water. I kicked with my feet while leaving my arms immobile by my side. I rocked and twirled rather than swam, my body feeling all of a piece. My belly was warm and full, and I felt a secret kinship with the seals. At home in the water, I dove and spun happily. Consciousness and its object seemed to be one; there was stillness in all of my motion.

"I know what I would call this," I wanted to say, the grip of language reasserting itself in my brain. But I did not know if Margaret would understand. "Finally," I thought, imagining the Buddha turning the wheel of the dharma. "The perfect lobster roll!"

Endnotes

Introduction

1. J. Chasseguet-Smirgel & B. Grunberger, *Freud or Reich? Psychoanalysis and Illusion*. New Haven & London: Yale University Press, 1986, p. 130.

2. Sigmund Freud, "Beyond the Pleasure Principle," in vol. 18 of *Standard Edition of the Complete Psychological Works of Sigmund Freud*, ed. and trans. James Strachey. London: Hogarth Press and Institute of Psychoanalysis, 1955, p. 42.

3. Jack Engler, personal communication, 11/03.

4. Sigmund Freud, *Civilization and Its Discontents*, in vol. 21 of *Standard Edition of the Complete Psychological Works of Sigmund Freud*, ed. and trans. James Strachey. London: Hogarth Press and Institute of Psychoanalysis, 1961, p. 106.

5. Ian A. Baker, *The Dalai Lama's Secret Temple: Tantric Wall Paintings from Tibet*. New York: Thames and Hudson, 2000, p. 167.

6. Mark Epstein, *Going on Being*. New York: Broadway Books, 2001, pp. 1–2.

Chapter One

1. John Stevens, *Lust for Enlightenment: Buddhism and Sex*. Boston & London: Shambhala, 1990, p. 114.

2. William Buck, *Ramayana*. Berkeley and Los Angeles: University of California Press, 1976, p. 175.

3. Those who are familiar with the *Ramayana* will know that at the close of the story, Sita and Rama are once again separated. As the story goes, people in Rama's kingdom began spreading rumors about Sita's infidelity while imprisoned in Lanka. Unable to bear the shame, Rama banishes her to the forest. Most scholars believe that this chapter of the tale was added in later years, for conservative social reasons, and I have not made use of this ending in my retelling of the story.

4. S. Freud, "Findings, ideas, problems" (1941, 1938), *S.E.* Vol. 23 (1964), p. 300.

5. Richard J. Kohn, *Lord of the Dance: The Mani Rimdu Festival in Tibet and Nepal*. Albany: State University of New York Press, 2001, p. 24.

Chapter Two

1. Heinrich Dumoulin, *Zen Buddhism: A History: India and China*. New York: Macmillan Publishing Company, 1988, pp. 8–9.

2. Diana Eck, *Banaras: City of Light*. New York: Alfred A. Knopf, 1982, p. 306.

3. June Campbell, *Traveller in Space: Gender, Identity and Tibetan Buddhism*. New York & London: Continuum, 1996, 2002, p. 56.

4. Bhikkhu Nanamoli, *The Life of the Buddha According to the Pali Canon*. Kandy, Sri Lanka: Buddhist Publication Society, 1972, 1992, p. 42.

5. From a chapter entitled "Craving" in the *Dhammapada* translated by P. Lal. New York: Farrar, Strauss & Giroux, 1967, pp. 156–162.

6. Ian A. Baker, *The Dalai Lama's Secret Temple: Tantric Wall Paintings from Tibet*. New York: Thames and Hudson, 2000, p. 51.

7. Jessica Benjamin, *Like Subjects, Love Objects: Essays on Recognition and Sexual Difference*. New Haven & London: Yale University Press, 1995, p. 184.

8. D. Eck, op. cit., p. 78.

9. Ibid., p. 184.

Chapter Three

1. Norman Fischer, "Meditation and the artistic impulse," *Inquiring Mind*, Volume 18, #2. Spring 2002, p. 6.

2. Thanks to Joseph Goldstein for relaying this story.

3. Thanks to Zen Master Pat O'Hara for this version of the story.

4. Anne Carson, *Eros: The Bittersweet*. New York: Dalkey Archive Press, 1986, 1998, p. 3.

5. Ibid., p. 9

6. S. Freud (1909), "Analysis of a phobia in a five-year-old boy," *SE*, 10. London: Hogarth Press, 1955, p. 23.

7. S. Freud (1920), *Beyond the Pleasure Principle, S.E.* 18, p. 42.

8. S. Freud (1930), *Civilization and Its Discontents, S.E.* 21, p. 106.

9. Carson, op cit., p. 16.

10. This view is offered in a wall text at the Seattle Asian Art

Museum, where one of the aforementioned *yakshi* figures is on permanent display.

11. Thanks to Maribeth Graybill, Senior Curator of Asian Art at the University of Michigan Museum of Art, for her lecture at the Japan Society, April 14, 2003, "Where Parallels Meet: The Place of Art in the Transmission of Buddhism."

Chapter Four

1. Otto Kernberg, *Love Relations: Normality and Pathology.* New Haven: Yale University Press, 1995, p. 44.

2. Jack Kornfield, *A Path with Heart.* New York: Bantam, 1993.

Chapter Five

1. See, for instance, Jonathan Lear, *Love and Its Place in Nature.* New Haven: Yale University Press, 1990, p. 149.

2. Bhikkhu Nanamoli, *The Life of the Buddha According to the Pali Canon.* Kandy, Sri Lanka, 1972, 1992, p. 77.

Chapter Six

1. Daniel Goleman (narrator), *Destructive Emotions: How Can We Overcome Them?: A Scientific Dialogue with the Dalai Lama.* New York: Bantam Books, 2003, p. 161.

2. Wendy Doniger O'Flaherty, *Siva: The Erotic Ascetic.* Oxford: Oxford University Press. 1973, p. 312.

3. Marcel Proust, *Remembrance of Things Past—The Captive.* London, 1972, pp. 248–249.

4. Reprinted in *On Wings of Awe (A Machzor for Rosh Hashanah and Yom Kippur),* edited and translated by Rabbi Richard N.

Levy. Washington, D.C.: B'nai B'rith Hillel Foundation, 1985, p. 381.

Chapter Seven

1. D. W. Winnicott, *Playing and Reality*. London & New York: Routledge, 1971, p. 81.

2. Jessica Benjamin, *The Bonds of Love: Psychoanalysis, Feminism, and the Problem of Domination*. New York: Pantheon Books, 1988, pp. 86–87.

3. Janine Chasseguet-Smirgel, *Sexuality and Mind: The Role of the Father and the Mother in the Psyche*. New York & London: New York University Press, 1986, pp. 27–28.

4. Jessica Benjamin, *Like Subjects, Love Objects: Essays on Recognition and Sexual Difference*. New Haven & London: Yale University Press, 1995, p. 125.

5. David A. Slawson, *Secret Teachings in the Art of Japanese Gardens*. Tokyo, New York & London: Kodansha International, 1987, p. 116.

6. Ibid.

7. Jessica Benjamin, *The Bonds of Love*, pp. 126–131.

8. M. Masud R. Khan, "Ego-Orgasm in Bisexual Love," *International Review of Psycho-Analysis*, 1 1974: 143–149.

9. D. W. Winnicott, "Communicating and Not Communicating Leading to a Study of Certain Opposites," in *The Maturational Processes and the Facilitating Environment*. New York: International Universities Press, 1965, p. 186.

Chapter Eight

1. See the *Knopf Guide to Morocco*. New York: Borzoi Books, 1994, pp. 104–105.

2. Stories about Munindra from Jack Engler are used with Engler's permission and were relayed via personal communication in November of 2003. Joseph Goldstein's reminiscences may be found in the Spring 2004 issue of *Tricycle: The Buddhist Review* (volume XIII, #3), p. 55.

3. D. W. Winnicott, *Playing and Reality*. London & New York: Routledge, 1971, pp. 79–85.

4. Ibid., p. 55.

Chapter Nine

1. Bhikkhu Nanamoli, *The Life of the Buddha*. Kandy, Sri Lanka: Buddhist Publication Society, 1972, p. 37.

2. Miranda Shaw, *Passionate Enlightenment: Women in Tantric Buddhism*. Princeton, New Jersey: Princeton University Press, 1994, pp. 140–178.

3. Personal communication from Nadine Helstroffer describing his work, *Le Temps de la Voix*.

4. Miranda Shaw, op. cit., pp. 150–151.

5. Anne Carolyn Klein, *Meeting the Great Bliss Queen: Buddhists, Feminists, and the Art of the Self*. Boston: Beacon Press, 1995, p. 61.

6. Jack Engler, "Being somebody and being nobody: A re-examination of the understanding of self in psychoanalysis and Buddhism." In *Psychoanalysis and Buddhism: An Unfolding Dialogue*, Jeremy Safran (editor). Boston: Wisdom Publications, 2003, pp. 35–80.

7. Ibid., p. 66.

8. Ibid., p. 68.

9. Judith Simmer-Brown, *Dakini's Warm Breath: The Feminine Principle in Tibetan Buddhism*. Boston & London: Shambhala, 2001, p. 41.

10. Ibid., p. 43.

11. Adam Phillips, *Darwin's Worms*. New York: Basic Books, 2000. See also a recounting of this same vignette in my *Going to Pieces Without Falling Apart*. New York: Broadway Books, 1998, pp. 61–63.

12. Sigmund Freud, "On Transience," in vol. 14 of *Standard Edition of the Complete Psychological Works of Sigmund Freud*, ed. and trans. James Strachey. London: Hogarth Press and Institute of Psychoanalysis, 1959, pp. 305–306.

13. A. Phillips, op. cit., p. 26.

Chapter Ten

1. See Jonathan Lear's *Love and Its Place in Nature: A Philosophical Interpretation of Freudian Psychoanalysis*. New Haven & London: Yale University Press, 1990, p. 61. Lear quotes Freud and Breuer from *Studies on Hysteria*, SE, 2: 157.

2. Anne Carolyn Klein, *Meeting the Great Bliss Queen: Buddhists, Feminists, and the Art of the Self*. Boston: Beacon Press, 1995, p. 163.

3. James S. Grotstein, *Who is the Dreamer Who Dreams the Dream?: A Study of Psychic Presences*. Hillsdale, N.J. & London: The Analytic Press, 2000, p. xvi.

4. Ibid., p. xxiii.

5. *On Wings of Awe (A Machzor for Rosh Hashanah and Yom Kippur)*, edited and translated by Rabbi Richard N. Levy.

Washington, D.C.: B'nai B'rith Hillel Foundation, 1985,
p. 259.

6. Michael Eigen, *Ecstasy*. Middletown, Ct.: Wesleyan University
Press, 2001, p. 81.

7. Otto F. Kernberg, *Love Relations: Normality and Pathology*. New
Haven & London: Yale University Press, 1995, p. 44.

References

Abram, J. 1996. *The Language of Winnicott*. Northvale, N.J. & London: Jason Aronson.

Anderson, R. 2001. *Being Upright: Zen Meditation and the Bodhisattva Precepts*. Berkeley: Rodmell Press.

Baker, I. 2000. *The Dalai Lama's Secret Temple: Tantric Wall Paintings from Tibet*. New York: Thames & Hudson.

Barthes, R. 1978. *A Lover's Discourse*. New York: Hill & Wang.

Batchelor, S. 2000. *Verses From the Center*. New York: Riverhead Books.

Benjamin, J. 1988. *The Bonds of Love*. New York: Pantheon Books.

———— 1995. *Like Subjects, Love Objects*. New Haven & London: Yale University Press.

Bion, W. R. 1992. *Cogitations*. London: Karnac Books.

Buck, W. 1976. *Ramayana*. Illustrated by Shirley Triest, introduction by B. A. van Nooten. Berkeley & Los Angeles: University of California Press.

Calasso, R. 1998. *Ka: Stories of the Mind and Gods of India*. New York: Vintage Books.

——— 2001. *Literature and the Gods*. New York: Alfred A. Knopf.

Campbell, J. 1996/2002. *Traveller in Space: Gender, Identity and Tibetan Buddhism*. London: Continuum Press.

Carson, A. 1986/1998. *Eros: The Bittersweet*. Dalkey Archive Press.

Chasseguet-Smirgel, J, 1986. *Sexuality and Mind*. New York & London: New York University Press.

———, and Grunberger, B. 1986. *Freud or Reich? Psychoanalysis and Illusion*. New Haven & London: Yale University Press.

Cleary, T. 1998. *The Ecstasy of Enlightenment: Teachings of Natural Tantra*. York Beach, Maine: Samuel Weiser.

Conze, E. 1951/1975. *Buddhism: Its Essence and Development*. New York: Harper Colophon.

Corbin, H. 1969. *Alone with the Alone: Creative Imagination in the Sufism of Ibn'Arabi*. Bollingen Series XCI. Princeton, N.J.: Princeton University Press.

Cozort, Daniel. 1986. *Highest Yoga Tantra*. Ithaca, N.Y.: Snow Lion.

Danielou, A. 1979/1992. *Gods of Love and Ecstasy: The Traditions of Shiva and Dionysus*. Rochester, Vt.: Inner Traditions.

——— 1977/2001. *The Hindu Temple: Deification of Eroticism*. Rochester, Vt.: Inner Traditions.

Doniger, W. & Kakar, S. 2002. *Kamasutra*. Oxford & New York: Oxford University Press.

Dumoulin, H. 1988. *Zen Buddhism: A History: India and China*. New York: Macmillan Publishing Company.

Eck, D. 1982. *Banaras: City of Light*. New York: Alfred A. Knopf.

Eigen, M. 2001. *Damaged Bonds*. London & New York: Karnac Press.

——— 2001. *Ecstasy*. Middletown, Ct.: Wesleyan University Press.

Faure, B. 1998. *The Red Thread: Buddhist Approaches to Sexuality*.

Princeton, N.J.: Princeton University Press.

Fisher, R. 1993. *Buddhist Art and Architecture*. London: Thames & Hudson.

Fonagy, P. 2001. *Attachment Theory and Psychoanalysis*. New York: Other Press.

Freud, S. All references are to *The Standard Edition of the Complete Psychological Works of Sigmund Freud (SE)*, vols. 1–24, ed. J. Strachey. London: Hogarth Press, 1953–74.

———— 1895. *Studies in Hysteria. SE* 2.

———— 1909. "Analysis of a phobia in a five-year-old boy," *SE* 10: 3–148.

———— 1920. *Beyond the Pleasure Principle. SE* 18:1–64.

———— 1930. *Civilization and Its Discontents. SE* 21: 59–145.

———— 1941. "Findings, ideas, problems." *SE* 23: 299–300.

Goldman, R. 1984/1990. *The Ramayana of Valmiki*. Princeton, N.J.: Princeton University Press.

Goleman, D. 2003. *Destructive Emotions: How Can We Overcome Them?: A Scientific Dialogue with the Dalai Lama*. New York: Bantam Books.

Green, A. 2000. *Chains of Eros: The Sexual in Psychoanalysis*. London: Rebus Press.

Grotstein, J. 2000. *Who is the Dreamer Who Dreams the Dream?* Hillsdale, N.J. & London: Analytic Press.

Hopkins, J. 1998. *Sex, Orgasm, and the Mind of Clear Light: The Sixty-Four Arts of Gay Male Love*. Berkeley: North Atlantic Press.

———— 1992. *Tibetan Arts of Love: Sex, Orgasm and Spiritual Healing*. Ithaca, N.Y.: Snow Lion Publications.

Humphreys, C. 1987. *The Wisdom of Buddhism*. London: Curzon Press.

Ingalls, D. 1965/2000. *Sanskrit Poetry: From Vidyakara's "Treasury."* Cambridge: Harvard University Press.

Jung, C. 1933. *Modern Man in Search of a Soul*. New York: Harcourt, Brace & World.

Kernberg, O. 1995. *Love Relations: Normality and Pathology*. New Haven & London: Yale University Press.

Klein, A. 1995. *Meeting the Great Bliss Queen: Buddhists, Feminists, and the Art of the Self*. Boston: Beacon Press.

Knox, R. 1992. *Amaravati: Buddhist Sculpture from the Great Stupa*. London: British Museum Press.

Kohn, R. 2001. *Lord of the Dance: The Mani Rimdu Festival in Tibet and Nepal*. Albany: State University of New York Press.

Kornfield, J. 1993. *A Path with Heart*. New York: Bantam Books.

Lal, P. 1967. *The Dhammapada*. New York: Farrar, Strauss & Giroux.

——— 1989. *The Ramayana of Valmiki*. New Delhi: Vikas Publishing House.

Lear, J. 1990. *Love and Its Place in Nature: A Philosophical Interpretation of Freudian Psychoanalysis*. New Haven & London: Yale University Press.

Levinas, E. 1982/1985. *Ethics and Infinity*. Richard Cohen, trans. Pittsburgh: Duquesne University Press.

——— 1982/2003. *On Escape*. Bettina Bergo, trans. Stanford, Calif.: Stanford University Press.

———1961/2001. *Totality and Infinity*. Alphonso Lingis, trans. Pittsburgh: Duquesne University Press.

Loewald, H. 1988. *Sublimation*. New Haven & London: Yale University Press.

Menzies, J. 2001. *Buddha: Radiant Awakening*. Sydney: Art Gallery of New South Wales.

Mitchell, S. 2002. *Can Love Last? The Fate of Romance Over Time*. New York & London: W. W. Norton.

Nanamoli, B. 1972/1992. *The Life of the Buddha*. Kandy, Sri Lanka: Buddhist Publication Society.

Odier, D. 1999/2001. *Desire: The Tantric Path to Awakening*. Rochester, Vt.: Inner Traditions.

O'Flaherty, W. 1973. *Siva: The Erotic Ascetic*. Oxford & New York: Oxford University Press.

Paz, O. 1993/1995. *The Double Flame: Love and Eroticism*. Helen Lane, trans. San Diego, New York & London: Harcourt, Brace & Company.

Phillips, A. 1993. *On Kissing, Tickling and Being Bored*. Cambridge: Harvard University Press.

——— 1996. *Terrors and Experts*. Cambridge: Harvard University Press.

——— 2000. *Darwin's Worms*. New York: Basic Books.

Rahula, W. 1959/1974. *What the Buddha Taught*. New York: Grove Press.

Rawson, P. 1981. *Oriental Erotic Art*. New York: Gallery Books.

Reps, P. 1989. *Zen Flesh, Zen Bones*. New York: Anchor Books.

Safran, J. 2003. *Psychoanalysis and Buddhism*. Boston: Wisdom Publications.

Shaw, M. 1994. *Passionate Enlightenment*. Princeton, N.J.: Princeton University Press.

Simmer-Brown, J. 2001. *Dakini's Warm Breath: The Feminine Principle in Tibetan Buddhism*. Boston: Shambhala Publications.

Slawson, D. 1987. *Secret Teachings In the Art of Japanese Gardens*. Tokyo, New York & London: Kodansha International.

Snodgrass, A. 1985. *The Symbolism of the Stupa*. Ithaca, N.Y.: Southeast Asia Program.

Stevens, J. 1990. *Lust for Enlightenment: Buddhism and Sex*. Boston & London: Shambhala Publications.

Strong, J. 1995. *The Experience of Buddhism*. Belmont, Calif.: Wadsworth Publishing Company.

Theweleit, K. 1990/1994. *Object-Choice: (All you need is love . . .)*. London & New York: Verso.

Thurman, R. 1995. *Essential Tibetan Buddhism*. San Francisco: HarperSanFrancisco.

Trungpa, C. 1973. *Cutting Through Spiritual Materialism*. Berkeley: Shambhala Publications.

Verhaeghe, P. 1999. *Love in a Time of Loneliness*. New York: Other Press.

Winnicott, D. W. 1965/1991. *The Maturational Processes and the Facilitating Environment*. Madison, Ct.: International Universities Press.

———— 1971/1989. *Playing and Reality*. London & New York: Routledge.

Index

meditation *(continued)*
 left-handed path and, 96, 165
 movement from object to
  subject, 171
 of Shiva, 119
 as tool of Buddhism, 162
 vipassana ("insight"
  meditation), 116–17
Middle Path, 14, 38–41
miegakure ("hide-and-reveal"), 138
mind-to-mind transmission, 36
monks, 43, 166–67
monuments *(stupas)*, 73–77, 145,
 149, 174
Moses, 188–90
mourning, 111, 177
Munindra, Anagarika
 Engler's instruction, 145–51,
  152, 153–54
 facilitating environment
  created, 159–60
Musil, Robert, 5

Nasruddin's parable, 1–3, 7, 9, 58,
 61
natural state, 171–72
Nietzsche, Friedrich, 11–12
nirvana, 63, 77, 167
Nisargadatta, Sri, 8
non-duality, 166, 172, 183

objectification
 attention to, 63–64
 of children, 123
 elimination of, 131–42, 170
 left-handed path and, 182
 in *Ramayana*, 29, 31, 33
orgasm
 as analogy, 56
 awakened mind and, 10

ego-orgasm, 138–39
 grace of, 170
otherness
 bliss of, 172
 desire and, 141
 female sexuality and, 173
 inaccessibility of, 171–72
 non-clinging and, 169
 passion and, 92

pace, 199–200
Padmasambhava, 14
parents
 of Buddha, 107–8
 children and, 105–6, 120–26,
  135–36, 194, 195
 psychoanalytic theory on
  family dynamics,
  134–36
 separation from, 151
Parvati, 120
passion, 91–92, 165, 170
penis envy, 135
phallus, 134–36, 194–95
Phillips, Adam, 176–77
Piaget, Jean, 156
Plato, 97
play, 151–60
possession, urge to claim
 compassion and, 197
 frustration associated with,
  68, 131
 limits to, 165
 love and, 58
 male desire and, 131, 183
 renunciation of, 126
The Prophet (Gibran), 126
Proust, Marcel, 124
psychoanalytic theory
 addressing clinging, 96, 181